MCQS OF C PROGRAMMING

1. **Which of the following is the correct syntax for declaring a variable in C?**
   - a) int variable;
   - b) variable int;
   - c) int; variable
   - d) variable; int

   Correct Answer a) int variable;

   This declares a variable named variable of type int.

2. **What is the size of the int data type in C (assuming a 32-bit system)?**
   - a) 2 bytes
   - b) 4 bytes
   - c) 8 bytes
   - d) 16 bytes

   Correct Answer: b) 4 bytes

3. **Which function is used to print text to the console in C?**
   - a) scanf()
   - b) printf()
   - c) print()
   - d) puts()

   correct answer is: b) printf()

To print text to the console in C, you use the printf function.

This function allows you to format and display data on the console.

4. **Which of the following is a correct way to initialize an array in C?**
    - a) int arr = {1, 2, 3};
    - b) int arr[3] = {1, 2, 3};
    - c) int arr[3] = [1, 2, 3];
    - d) int arr(3) = {1, 2, 3};

Correct Answer: b) int arr[3] = {1, 2, 3};

The correct way to initialize an array in C

It creates an array named arr of size 3 and initializes it with the values 1, 2, and 3.

5. **What is the output of the following code?**

```
int main() {
   int a = 5, b = 10;
   printf("%d", a+b);
   return 0;
}
```

   - a) 5
   - b) 10
   - c) 15
   - d) 0

correct answer is: c) 15

6. **Which of the following operators is used to access the value at the address stored in a pointer variable?**

- a) *
- b) &
- c) ->
- d) .

Correct Answer a) *

The operator used to access the value at the address stored in a pointer variable is the dereference operator.

This operator allows you to access the value that the pointer is pointing to.

7. **What does the continue statement do in a loop?**
    - a) Exits the loop
    - b) Skips the current iteration and proceeds with the next iteration
    - c) Restarts the loop from the beginning
    - d) None of the above

correct answer

b) Skips the current iteration and proceeds with the next iteration

The continue statement is used to skip the current iteration of a loop and proceed with the next iteration. It does not exit the loop or restart it from the beginning.

8. **Which keyword is used to define a structure in C?**
    - a) struct
    - b) class
    - c) define
    - d) typedef

9. **Which of the following is true about dynamic memory allocation in C?**
    - a) malloc returns a pointer to the allocated memory
    - b) calloc initializes the allocated memory to zero

- c) realloc changes the size of previously allocated memory
- d) All of the above

Answer: d) All of the above

- **Explanation:**
  - malloc indeed returns a pointer to the allocated memory.
  - calloc initializes the allocated memory to zero.
  - realloc changes the size of previously allocated memory.

10. **What will be the output of the following code?**

```
#include <stdio.h>
void main() {
    char str[] = "Hello";
    printf("%s", str);
}
```

- a) H
- b) He
- c) Hel
- d) Hello

Answer: d) Hello

- **Explanation:**
  - The printf function with %s format specifier prints the entire string stored in the character array str. Since str contains "Hello", it outputs Hello.

11. **Which of the following is a correct statement about the static keyword in C?**
    - a) It makes a variable persist for the duration of the program

- b) It restricts the visibility of a variable to the current file
- c) It changes the linkage of a variable to internal
- d) All of the above

Answer: d) All of the above

- **Explanation:**
  - A static variable persists for the duration of the program.
  - static restricts the visibility of a variable to the current file (when used in global scope).
  - It changes the linkage of a global variable or function to internal, preventing external linkage.

12. **What does the sizeof operator return?**
    - a) The size of the data type in bytes
    - b) The length of a string
    - c) The number of elements in an array
    - d) None of the above

Answer: a) The size of the data type in bytes

- **Explanation:**
  - sizeof returns the size (in bytes) of a data type or a variable. It does not calculate the length of a string or the number of elements in an array.

13. **What is the output of the following code?**

```
int main() {
   int x = 10;
   if (x == 10) {
      printf("x is 10\n");
   }
   else {
```

```
        printf("x is not 10\n");
    }
    return 0;
}
```

- a) x is 10
- b) x is not 10
- c) Compiler error
- d) Runtime error

Explanation:

- The variable x is initialized to 10.
- The condition if (x == 10) evaluates to true.
- The printf("x is 10\n"); statement inside the if block is executed.

Correct Answer:
a) x is 10

14. **Which of the following is not a valid storage class in C?**
    - a) auto
    - b) register
    - c) static
    - d) public

Correct Answer:
d) public

Explanation:

- auto, register, and static are valid storage classes in C.
    - auto: Default storage class for local variables.
    - register: Suggests storing the variable in a CPU register for faster access.

- static: Preserves the variable value across function calls or provides internal linkage for global variables.
- public is not a storage class in C (it exists in some other languages like C++ for access specifiers).

15. **Which of the following is used to create a loop that runs exactly once?**
    - a) for
    - b) while
    - c) do-while
    - d) None of the above

The correct loop to use if you want to ensure it runs at least once is:

c) do-while

The do-while loop executes the block of code once before checking the condition at the end, ensuring the loop runs at least one time.

16. **What will be the output of the following code?**

```
int main() {
   int a = 5;
   printf("%d %d %d", a++, a++, a++);
   return 0;
}
```

- a) 5 6 7
- b) 7 6 5
- c) 7 7 7
- d) Undefined behavior

The given code involves using the post-increment operator (a++) multiple times within the same printf statement. This can lead to undefined behavior because the order of evaluation of the operands is not specified in this case.

So, the correct answer is:

d) Undefined behavior

17. **What is the correct way to declare a function pointer in C?**
    - a) int *func()
    - b) int (func)()
    - c) int func*()
    - d) int (*func)

The correct way to declare a function pointer in C is:

b) int (func)()

This syntax declares func as a pointer to a function that returns an int and takes no parameters.

18. **What will be the output of the following code?**

```
#include <stdio.h>
int main() {
   char ch = 'A';
   printf("%d", ch);
   return 0;
}
```

- a) A
- b) 65
- c) 97
- d) Compiler error

The character 'A' has an ASCII value of 65. The printf function with the %d format specifier will print the integer value of the character.

So, the correct answer is: **b) 65**

19. **Which of the following functions is used to dynamically allocate memory for an array in C?**
    - a) malloc
    - b) calloc
    - c) realloc
    - d) alloc

The function used to dynamically allocate memory for an array in C and also initialize it to zero is:

b) calloc

The calloc function allocates memory for an array of a specified number of elements and initializes all the allocated memory to zero.

20. **What is the purpose of the #include preprocessor directive in C?**
    - a) To define macros
    - b) To include standard library functions
    - c) To conditionally compile code
    - d) To terminate the program

The purpose of the #include preprocessor directive in C is:

b) To include standard library functions

This directive allows you to include the contents of a file or a library into your program before the compilation process begins. It is commonly used to include standard library headers like stdio.h for input and output functions.

21. **What does the following code output?**

```
#include <stdio.h>
#define SQUARE(x) x * x
int main() {
    int a = 3;
    printf("%d", SQUARE(a+1));
    return 0;
```

```
}
```

- a) 16
- b) 9
- c) 12
- d) Compiler error

The macro SQUARE(x) is defined as x * x. When you call SQUARE(a+1), it expands to (a+1) * (a+1) without parentheses around the expression. This results in the expression a + 1 * a + 1, which evaluates to 3 + 1 * 3 + 1, following the order of operations (multiplication before addition). So the result is 3 + 3 + 1, which equals 7.

Thus, the output is:

c) 12

22. **Which keyword is used to prevent a variable from being modified in C?**
    - a) const
    - b) volatile
    - c) static
    - d) register

The keyword used to prevent a variable from being modified in C is:

a) const

This keyword ensures that the variable's value cannot be changed after it is initialized.

23. **What is the output of the following code?**

```
#include <stdio.h>
int main() {
    int a = 10;
    int b = 5;
    printf("%d", a && b);
```

```
    return 0;
}
```

- a) 1
- b) 0
- c) 5
- d) 10

uses the logical AND operator (&&). In C, the logical AND operator returns 1 if both operands are non-zero and 0 if either is zero. Since both a (10) and b (5) are non-zero, the expression a && b evaluates to 1.

So, the correct answer is:

a) 1

24. **Which function is used to deallocate the memory allocated by** malloc **in C?**
    - a) delete
    - b) remove
    - c) free
    - d) dealloc

The function used to deallocate memory allocated by malloc in C is:

c) free

This function releases the allocated memory, preventing memory leaks and ensuring efficient memory management.

25. **What is the output of the following code?**

```
int main() {
    int a = 3;
    printf("%d\n", a << 1);
    return 0;
}
```

- a) 1
- b) 3
- c) 6
- d) 9

Answer: c) 6
Explanation: The << operator is the left shift operator. It shifts the bits of a to the left by 1 position, which is equivalent to multiplying a by 2. For a = 3 (binary 0011), a << 1 results in 6 (binary 0110).

26. **Which header file is required to use the** malloc **function in C?**
    - a) <stdlib.h>
    - b) <stdio.h>
    - c) <string.h>
    - d) <math.h>

Answer: a) <stdlib.h>
Explanation: The malloc function is defined in the <stdlib.h> header file, which is used for memory allocation and process control.

27. **What is the correct way to check if a number is even in C?**
    - a) if (number / 2 == 0)
    - b) if (number % 2 == 0)
    - c) if (number & 1 == 0)
    - d) if (number - 2 == 0)

Answer: b) if (number % 2 == 0)
Explanation: The modulus operator % returns the remainder of a division. If the remainder of dividing a number by 2 is 0, the number is even.

28. **Which of the following is true about function pointers in C?**
    - a) They can store the address of a function
    - b) They can be passed as arguments to other functions

- c) They can be returned from functions
- d) All of the above

Answer: d) All of the above
Explanation: Function pointers in C can:

- Store the address of a function.
- Be passed as arguments to other functions.
- Be returned from functions.

29. **What will be the output of the following code?**

```
#include <stdio.h>
int main() {
    int a = 5, b = 15;
    printf("%d", a^b);
    return 0;
}
```

- a) 10
- b) 20
- c) 0
- d) 25

Answer: a) 10
Explanation:
The ^ operator is the **bitwise XOR** operator. XOR returns 1 if the bits are different and 0 if they are the same.
Binary for 5 = 0101 and 15 = 1111.
0101 ^ 1111 = 1010 (which is 10 in decimal).

30. **Which of the following is used to prevent multiple inclusions of the same header file in C?**
    - a) #include
    - b) #define
    - c) #ifdef
    - d) #ifndef

Answer: d) #ifndef

Explanation:
The #ifndef (if not defined) directive is used to create include guards. Combined with #define, it ensures the header file is only included once.

31. What is the output of the following code?

```c
#include <stdio.h>
int main() {
    int arr[] = {1, 2, 3, 4, 5};
    int *p = arr;
    printf("%d", *(p+3));
    return 0;
}
```

- a) 1
- b) 2
- c) 3
- d) 4

Answer: d) 4
Explanation:
p points to the first element of the array (arr[0]). Adding 3 to p makes it point to arr[3], which is 4.

32. What is the purpose of the fopen function in C?
- a) To open a file
- b) To close a file
- c) To read from a file
- d) To write to a file

Answer: a) To open a file
Explanation:
The fopen function is used to open a file and returns a pointer to the file.

33. What will be the output of the following code?

```c
#include <stdio.h>
int main() {
    int x = 2;
```

```
    printf("%d", x *= 3 + 2);
    return 0;
}
```

- a) 10
- b) 12
- c) 16
- d) 8

Answer: a) 10
Explanation:
The *= operator applies multiplication after evaluating the right-hand side. x *= 3 + 2 is equivalent to x = x * (3 + 2) = 2 * 5 = 10.

34. **What is the result of the following expression: 5 & 3?**
    - a) 1
    - b) 2
    - c) 3
    - d) 5

Answer: b) 1
Explanation:
The & operator is the **bitwise AND** operator.
Binary for 5 = 0101 and 3 = 0011.
0101 & 0011 = 0001 (which is 1 in decimal).

35. **What does the void keyword indicate when used in a function declaration in C?**
    - a) The function returns no value
    - b) The function returns a value
    - c) The function is inline
    - d) The function is static

Answer: a) The function returns no value
Explanation:
The void keyword specifies that a function does not return any value.

36. **Which of the following is a valid way to declare a union in C?**
    - a) union { int a; float b; };
    - b) union data { int a; float b; };
    - c) union data { int a, float b; };
    - d) union { int a, float b; };

Answer: b) union data { int a; float b; };
Explanation:
The correct syntax for declaring a union in C requires defining a name for the union (data) and separating its members with semicolons.

37. **Which function is used to write a formatted string to a file in C?**
    - a) fwrite()
    - b) fprintf()
    - c) fscanf()
    - d) fgets()

Answer: b) fprintf()
Explanation:
The fprintf function allows formatted output to a file, similar to how printf works for console output.

38. **What is the correct way to declare a constant variable in C?**
    - a) const int x;
    - b) int x const;
    - c) constant int x;
    - d) int constant x;

Answer: a) const int x;
Explanation:
The const keyword is used to declare a variable as constant, meaning its value cannot be changed.

39. **What is the output of the following code?**

```
#include <stdio.h>
int main() {
```

```
    char *ptr = "Hello";
    printf("%c", *ptr);
    return 0;
}
```

- a) H
- b) e
- c) o
- d) l

Answer: a) H
Explanation:
*ptr dereferences the pointer to the first character of the string "Hello", which is 'H'.

40. **Which of the following operators is used for bitwise OR in C?**
    - a) |
    - b) &
    - c) ^
    - d) ~

Answer: a) |
Explanation:
The | operator performs a **bitwise OR**, returning 1 if either of the bits is 1.

Intermediate Level MCQs

41. **What will be the output of the following code?**

```
int main() {
    int x = 5;
    int y = x > 0 ? x : -x;
    printf("%d", y);
    return 0;
}
```

- a) 5
- b) -5
- c) 0
- d) -1

Answer: a) 5

Explanation:

The ternary operator ? : is a shorthand for an if-else statement.

The condition x > 0 evaluates to true because x is 5.

Thus, the value of y becomes x, which is 5.

42. **Which of the following correctly declares a two-dimensional array in C?**
    - a) int arr[2][3];
    - b) int arr[2, 3];
    - c) int arr(2)(3);
    - d) int arr[2][3];

Answer: a) int arr[2][3];

Explanation:

The correct syntax to declare a two-dimensional array is int arr[rows][columns];.

43. **What is the output of the following code?**

```
int main() {
   int a = 1, b = 2, c = 3;
   int d = (a, b, c);
   printf("%d", d);
   return 0;
}
```

- a) 1
- b) 2

- c) 3
- d) Compiler error

Answer: c) 3

Explanation:

The comma operator evaluates its operands from left to right and returns the value of the last operand.

(a, b, c) evaluates a, then b, then c, and assigns the value of c (3) to d.

44. **What is the correct way to check if a pointer is NULL in C?**
    - a) if (ptr == NULL)
    - b) if (ptr == 0)
    - c) if (!ptr)
    - d) All of the above

- **Answer: d) All of the above**
  Explanation:
  All the provided methods are valid for checking if a pointer is NULL:

1. if (ptr == NULL) explicitly checks against the NULL macro.
2. if (ptr == 0) works because NULL is typically defined as 0.
3. if (!ptr) works because NULL is evaluated as false in boolean contexts.

45. **What will be the output of the following code?**

```
#include <stdio.h>
int main() {
   int a = 5, b = 10;
   printf("%d %d", a++, ++b);
   return 0;
}
```

- a) 5 10
- b) 6 11
- c) 5 11
- d) 6 10

Answer: c) 5 11

Explanation:

The a++ post-increment operator returns the value of a before incrementing, so 5 is printed.

The ++b pre-increment operator increments b first and then returns the new value, so 11 is printed.

46. What does the extern keyword signify in C?
- a) A variable is defined in another file
- b) A function is static
- c) A variable is local to the function
- d) A variable is constant

Answer: a) A variable is defined in another file
Explanation:
The extern keyword declares a variable or function without defining it, indicating that its definition exists elsewhere (e.g., in another file).

47. What is the output of the following code?

```
#include <stdio.h>
int main() {
    int a = 10;
    int *p = &a;
    printf("%d", *p);
    return 0;
}
```

- a) 0
- b) 10

- c) Address of a
- d) Runtime error

Answer: b) 10
Explanation:
The *p dereferences the pointer p, accessing the value stored at the memory address of a. Since a is 10, the output is 10.

48. **Which of the following is not a standard library function in C?**
    - a) strcat()
    - b) strcpy()
    - c) strrev()
    - d) strcmp()

Answer: c) strrev()
Explanation:
The strrev() function is not part of the standard C library. It is a non-standard function provided by some compilers.
The other functions, strcat(), strcpy(), and strcmp(), are standard string-handling functions.

49. **What does the restrict keyword mean in C?**
    - a) It indicates that a pointer is the only means of accessing a particular data object
    - b) It restricts the visibility of a variable to the current file
    - c) It restricts a function to be used within a single file
    - d) It makes a variable constant

Answer: a) It indicates that a pointer is the only means of accessing a particular data object
Explanation:
The restrict keyword is a promise to the compiler that the pointer is the sole access path to the data it points to, allowing optimization.
Other options are unrelated to the restrict keyword.

50. **What is the output of the following code?**

```c
#include <stdio.h>
void swap(int *a, int *b) {
    int temp = *a;
    *a = *b;
    *b = temp;
}
int main() {
    int x = 5, y = 10;
    swap(&x, &y);
    printf("%d %d", x, y);
    return 0;
}
```

- a) 5 10
- b) 10 5
- c) 0 0
- d) Runtime error

Answer: b) 10 5
Explanation:
The swap function exchanges the values of x and y by modifying their values through pointers. The updated values are 10 for x and 5 for y.

51. **Which of the following is a valid statement about inline functions in C?**
    - a) They suggest to the compiler to insert the code directly at the call site
    - b) They cannot contain loops
    - c) They are always faster than normal functions
    - d) All of the above

Answer: a) They suggest to the compiler to insert the code directly at the call site
Explanation:
The inline keyword hints to the compiler to replace the function call with its code to eliminate call overhead.

52. What is the output of the following code?

```c
#include <stdio.h>
int main() {
    int i;
    for (i = 0; i < 5; i++) {
        if (i == 3) break;
    }
    printf("%d", i);
    return 0;
}
```

- a) 2
- b) 3
- c) 4
- d) 5

Answer: b) 3

Explanation:
The loop runs from i = 0 to i < 5. When i == 3, the break statement terminates the loop. After the loop exits, i retains the value 3.

53. What is the result of the expression ~0 in C (assuming 32-bit representation)?

- a) -1
- b) 0
- c) 1
- d) 4294967295

Answer: a) -1

Explanation:

The ~ operator is the bitwise NOT operator, which inverts all bits. For a 32-bit integer, 0 in binary is 00000000...0000.

Applying ~ flips all bits, resulting in 11111111...1111, which is the two's complement representation of -1.

54. **Which of the following is a valid use of the** typedef **keyword in C?**
- a) typedef int integer;
- b) typedef struct { int x; } point;
- c) typedef int array[10];
- d) All of the above

Answer: d) All of the above

Explanation:

Option a): typedef int integer; creates an alias integer for int.

Option b): typedef struct { int x; } point; creates an alias point for an anonymous structure.

Option c): typedef int array[10]; creates an alias array for an array of size 10.

All are valid uses of typedef.

55. **What is the output of the following code?**

```
#include <stdio.h>
int main() {
   int x = 10;
   printf("%d %d", x++, ++x);
   return 0;
}
```

- a) 10 11
- b) 11 11
- c) 11 12
- d) Undefined behavior

Answer: d) Undefined behavior
Explanation:
The behavior is undefined because x is modified multiple times (x++ and ++x) without a sequence point in between. This violates the C standard rules for evaluating expressions.

56. What is the purpose of the #define directive in C?

- a) To create symbolic constants
- b) To define macros
- c) Both a and b
- d) None of the above

Answer: c) Both a and b

Explanation:

The #define directive is used to:

Create symbolic constants (e.g., #define PI 3.14).

Define macros for code substitution (e.g., #define SQUARE(x) ((x) * (x))).

57. What is the output of the following code?

```
int main() {
   int x = 7, y = 14;
   if (x > y) {
      printf("x is greater\n");
   } else {
      printf("y is greater\n");
   }
   return 0;
}
```

- a) x is greater
- b) y is greater
- c) x is greater or equal
- d) y is greater or equal

Answer: b) y is greater

Explanation:

The condition x > y evaluates to false because 7 is not greater than 14. The program executes the else block, printing "y is greater".

58. What does the following code print?

```
int main() {
    for (int i = 0; i < 3; i++) {
        for (int j = 0; j < 2; j++) {
            printf("%d%d\n", i, j);
        }
    }
    return 0;
}
```

- a) 00 10 11 10 20 21
- b) 00 01 10 11 21 20
- c) 00 01 10 11 20 21
- d) 00 10 11 10 20

Answer: c) 00 01 10 11 20 21
Explanation:
The outer loop (i) runs 3 times (0, 1, 2), and the inner loop (j) runs 2 times (0, 1) for each value of i.
The printf("%d%d\n", i, j) prints each combination of i and j, followed by a newline.

59. **Which function is used to convert a string to an integer in C?**
    - a) atoi()
    - b) atof()
    - c) strtol()
    - d) sprintf()

Answer: a) atoi()
Explanation:
The atoi() function converts a string to an integer.

60. **What is the output of the following code?**

```
int main() {
    int a = 5, b = 2;
    printf("%d", a / b);
    return 0;
}
```

- a) 2
- b) 2.5
- c) 3
- d) 2.0

Answer: a) 2

Explanation:

In C, dividing two integers (int) performs integer division, which discards the fractional part.

5 / 2 results in 2, with the remainder discarded.

61. What will be the output of the following code?

```
#include <stdio.h>
#define MAX(a, b) ((a) > (b) ? (a) : (b))
int main() {
    int x = 5, y = 10;
    printf("%d", MAX(x, y));
    return 0;
}
```

- a) 5
- b) 10
- c) 15
- d) Runtime error

Answer: b) 10

Explanation:

The macro MAX(a, b) uses the ternary operator to evaluate (x > y) ? x : y. Since y = 10 is greater, the output is 10.

62. What is the result of the following expression: (5 > 3) && (8 > 5)?

- a) 1

- b) 0
- c) True
- d) False

Answer: a) 1

Explanation:

The && operator evaluates to 1 (true) if both conditions are true.

5 > 3 is true (1), and 8 > 5 is true (1). Therefore, the result is 1.

63. **Which of the following correctly defines a recursive function in C?**
    - a) A function that calls itself
    - b) A function that returns a pointer
    - c) A function that allocates memory dynamically
    - d) A function that uses file operations

Answer: a) A function that calls itself
Explanation:
A recursive function is one that invokes itself in its body to solve smaller instances of the same problem.

64. **What is the output of the following code?**

```
#include <stdio.h>
int main() {
    int arr[5] = {1, 2, 3, 4, 5};
    int *ptr = arr;
    printf("%d", *(ptr + 2));
    return 0;
}
```

- a) 1
- b) 2
- c) 3
- d) 4

Answer: c) 3

Explanation:

The pointer ptr points to the first element of the array. Adding 2 to ptr moves it to the third element (arr[2]), which is 3.

65. What does the following code snippet demonstrate?

```
#include <stdio.h>
int main() {
    int a = 1;
    {
        int a = 2;
        printf("%d ", a);
    }
    printf("%d", a);
    return 0;
}
```

- a) Global and local scope
- b) Block scope and function scope
- c) Block scope and variable shadowing
- d) Variable shadowing and parameter passing

Answer: c) Block scope and variable shadowing

Explanation:

The inner block has its own variable a, which shadows the outer block's a.

Inside the block, 2 is printed. Outside, the outer a = 1 is printed.

66. What will be the output of the following code?

```
#include <stdio.h>
int main() {
    int x = 5;
    printf("%d", x == 5 ? 1 : 0);
    return 0;
```

}

- a) 0
- b) 1
- c) 5
- d) None of the above

Answer: b) 1
Explanation:
The ternary operator evaluates x == 5, which is true. Therefore, the result is 1.

67. **Which function is used to copy a string in C?**
    - a) strcpy()
    - b) strcat()
    - c) strcmp()
    - d) strlen()

Answer: a) strcpy()

Explanation:

The strcpy() function copies one string into another.

strcat() concatenates strings.

strcmp() compares strings.

strlen() calculates the length of a string.

68. **What is the output of the following code?**

```c
#include <stdio.h>
int main() {
    int a = 10, b = 5;
    int *ptr;
    ptr = &a;
    printf("%d", *ptr);
    ptr = &b;
    printf(" %d", *ptr);
    return 0;
}
```

- a) 10 5
- b) 5 10
- c) 0 0
- d) Runtime error

Answer: a) 10 5
Explanation:
The pointer ptr first points to a, so *ptr dereferences to 10. Then, it points to b, so *ptr dereferences to 5.

69. **What will be the output of the following code?**

```
#include <stdio.h>
int main() {
   int a[3] = {1, 2, 3};
   int *p = a;
   printf("%d", p[2]);
   return 0;
}
```

- a) 1
- b) 2
- c) 3
- d) Compiler error

Answer: c) 3
Explanation:
The pointer p behaves like an array. p[2] accesses the third element of the array, which is 3.

70. **What is the purpose of the void keyword in a function parameter list?**
    - a) It indicates the function does not take any parameters
    - b) It indicates the function returns nothing
    - c) It indicates the function has a variable number of parameters

- d) It indicates the function is a macro

Answer: a) It indicates the function does not take any parameters

Explanation:

In a function parameter list, void specifies that the function accepts no arguments.

In the return type, void means the function does not return a value.

71. **What will be the output of the following code?**

```
int main() {
    int a = 10;
    int b = 20;
    int c = a > b ? a : b;
    printf("%d", c);
    return 0;
}
```

- a) 10
- b) 20
- c) 30
- d) 0

Answer: b) 20

Explanation:

The ternary operator ? checks the condition a > b.

Since 10 > 20 is false, the value of b (20) is assigned to c. Therefore, the output is 20.

72. **Which of the following is a correct way to define a macro in C?**
- a) #define MAX 100
- b) int MAX = 100
- c) MAX = 100

- d) const int MAX = 100

Answer: a) #define MAX 100

Explanation:
The #define directive is used to define macros, which are preprocessor constants.

73. **What will be the output of the following code?**

```
int main() {
    char ch = 'A';
    printf("%c", ch + 1);
    return 0;
}
```

- a) A
- b) B
- c) 65
- d) 66

Answer: b) B
Explanation:
The character 'A' has an ASCII value of 65. Adding 1 results in 66, which corresponds to 'B'. The %c format specifier converts the value back to a character for output.

74. **Which operator is used to get the address of a variable in C?**
- a) *
- b) &
- c) @
- d) #

Answer: b) &
Explanation:
The & operator retrieves the memory address of a variable.

75. **What will be the output of the following code?**

```
#include <stdio.h>
int main() {
    int i = 0;
    while (i < 3) {
        printf("%d", i);
        i++;
    }
    return 0;
}
```

- a) 012
- b) 123
- c) 0123
- d) 321

Answer: a) 012
Explanation:
The while loop iterates while i < 3, printing the value of i (0, 1, 2) before incrementing.

76. **What is the purpose of the** malloc **function in C?**
    - a) To allocate memory dynamically
    - b) To free allocated memory
    - c) To initialize a variable
    - d) To allocate memory statically

Answer: a) To allocate memory dynamically
Explanation:
malloc dynamically allocates memory during runtime and returns a pointer to the allocated memory.

77. **What does the** static **keyword mean when used in a global variable declaration in C?**
    - a) The variable is visible only within the file it is declared
    - b) The variable is visible within all files

- c) The variable value cannot be changed
- d) The variable is initialized to zero

Answer: a) The variable is visible only within the file it is declared
Explanation:
A static global variable has **file scope**, limiting its visibility to the file it is declared in.

78. What is the output of the following code?

```
#include <stdio.h>
int main() {
    int arr[] = {10, 20, 30};
    printf("%d", sizeof(arr)/sizeof(arr[0]));
    return 0;
}
```

- a) 10
- b) 3
- c) 30
- d) 6

Answer: b) 3
Explanation:
sizeof(arr) gives the total size of the array in bytes, and sizeof(arr[0]) gives the size of one element. Dividing them gives the number of elements: 3.

79. Which function is used to find the length of a string in C?

- a) strlen()
- b) strcpy()
- c) strcat()
- d) strcmp()

Answer: a) strlen()
Explanation:
strlen() returns the number of characters in a string, excluding the null terminator.

80. **What is the correct way to declare a pointer to an integer in C?**
    - a) int *ptr;
    - b) int ptr*;
    - c) *int ptr;
    - d) ptr int*;

Answer: *a) int *ptr;*
Explanation:
The syntax int *ptr; declares ptr as a pointer to an int.

81. **What will be the output of the following code?**

```
#include <stdio.h>
void func(int x, int y) {
   x = x + y;
   y = x - y;
   x = x - y;
   printf("%d %d", x, y);
}
int main() {
   int a = 5, b = 10;
   func(a, b);
   return 0;
}
```

- a) 5 10
- b) 10 5
- c) 15 5
- d) 0 0

Answer: a) 5 10
Explanation:
The function swaps x and y internally, but since parameters are passed by value, the changes do not affect a and b in main().

82. **Which of the following is true about the** exit() **function in C?**

- a) It terminates the program execution
- b) It returns control to the operating system
- c) It can be used to indicate success or failure
- d) All of the above

Answer: d) All of the above
Explanation:
The exit() function:

1. Terminates program execution.
2. Returns control to the operating system.
3. Can indicate success (0) or failure (non-zero).

83. **What is the purpose of the** assert() **function in C?**
    - a) To test assumptions made by the program
    - b) To log messages
    - c) To allocate memory
    - d) To read from a file

Answer: a) To test assumptions made by the program
Explanation:
assert() halts program execution if a given condition is false, useful for debugging.

84. **What will be the output of the following code?**

```
#include <stdio.h>
int main() {
   int i = 1;
   do {
      printf("%d", i);
      i++;
   } while (i <= 3);
   return 0;
}
```

- a) 123
- b) 321

- c) 012
- d) 111

Answer: a) 123
Explanation:
The do-while loop runs at least once, printing 1, 2, and 3.

85. **What is the result of the following expression: 5 | 3?**
    - a) 1
    - b) 2
    - c) 7
    - d) 8

Answer: c) 7

Explanation:

The | operator is the bitwise OR operator.

Binary for 5: 0101

Binary for 3: 0011

0101 | 0011 = 0111, which is 7.

86. **Which of the following is the correct syntax to declare a function prototype in C?**
    - a) int func(int, int);
    - b) int func;
    - c) function int func(int, int);
    - d) int func(int int);

Answer: a) int func(int, int);
Explanation:
The correct function prototype specifies the return type, name, and parameter types: int func(int, int);.

87. **What is the output of the following code?**

```
#include <stdio.h>
int main() {
   int a = 5;
   printf("%d", a == 5 && a < 10);
   return 0;
```

}

- a) 0
- b) 1
- c) 5
- d) 10

Answer: b) 1

Explanation:

The logical AND (&&) operator evaluates both conditions:

a == 5 is true.

a < 10 is true.

The result is 1.

88. **Which of the following is used to allocate memory for an array dynamically in C?**
    - a) calloc()
    - b) malloc()
    - c) realloc()
    - d) All of the above

Answer: d) All of the above

Explanation:

malloc() and calloc() allocate memory dynamically.

realloc() reallocates memory dynamically.

89. **What is the purpose of the fseek() function in C?**
    - a) To move the file pointer to a specific location
    - b) To open a file
    - c) To close a file
    - d) To read from a file

Answer: a) To move the file pointer to a specific location
Explanation:
fseek() changes the position of the file pointer within a

file.

90. What will be the output of the following code?

```
#include <stdio.h>
int main() {
    char *str = "Hello";
    printf("%c", *str);
    return 0;
}
```

- a) H
- b) e
- c) o
- d) l

Answer: a) H
Explanation:
The pointer str points to the first character of the string "Hello". The dereference operator (*) accesses the value, which is 'H'.

91. What is the difference between malloc() and calloc() in C?

- a) malloc() allocates memory without initializing it, calloc() initializes it to zero
- b) calloc() allocates memory without initializing it, malloc() initializes it to zero
- c) malloc() and calloc() both allocate memory and initialize it
- d) malloc() and calloc() both allocate memory without initializing it

Answer: a) malloc() allocates memory without initializing it, calloc() initializes it to zero

Explanation:

malloc() allocates memory without initializing it.

calloc() allocates and initializes the memory to zero.

92. What will be the output of the following code?

```c
#include <stdio.h>
int main() {
    int x = 5, y = 3;
    x = x ^ y;
    y = x ^ y;
    x = x ^ y;
    printf("%d %d", x, y);
    return 0;
}
```

- a) 5 3
- b) 3 5
- c) 0 0
- d) Runtime error

Answer: b) 3 5
Explanation:
This code swaps the values of x and y using the XOR operation.

93. **What is the purpose of the feof() function in C?**
    - a) To check if the end of a file has been reached
    - b) To open a file
    - c) To close a file
    - d) To read from a file

Answer: a) To check if the end of a file has been reached
Explanation:
feof() checks whether the end of a file has been reached during reading.

94. **What is the output of the following code?**

```c
#include <stdio.h>
int main() {
    int a = 10;
    if (a > 0) {
        printf("Positive\n");
```

```
    } else {
        printf("Negative\n");
    }
    return 0;
}
```

- a) Positive
- b) Negative
- c) 0
- d) Runtime error

Answer: a) Positive
Explanation:
The condition a > 0 is true, so "Positive" is printed.

95. **Which function is used to compare two strings in C?**
    - a) strcmp()
    - b) strcpy()
    - c) strcat()
    - d) strchr()

Answer: a) strcmp()
Explanation:
strcmp() compares two strings lexicographically.

96. **What is the output of the following code?**

```
#include <stdio.h>
int main() {
    int x = 1;
    switch (x) {
        case 1:
            printf("One\n");
            break;
        case 2:
            printf("Two\n");
            break;
        default:
```

```
            printf("None\n");
            break;
    }
    return 0;
}
```

- a) One
- b) Two
- c) None
- d) Runtime error

Answer: a) One
Explanation:
The switch statement matches x = 1 with case 1 and prints "One". The break prevents further execution.

97. **What will be the output of the following code?**

```
int main() {
    int x = 0;
    for (x = 1; x <= 5; x++) {
        printf("%d", x);
    }
    return 0;
}
```

- a) 01234
- b) 12345
- c) 54321
- d) 23456

Answer: b) 12345
Explanation:
The for loop starts with x = 1 and runs until x <= 5, printing 1, 2, 3, 4, and 5 consecutively.

98. **Which of the following correctly describes a NULL pointer?**

- a) A pointer that points to an uninitialized variable
- b) A pointer that is not pointing to any memory location
- c) A pointer that points to a deleted variable
- d) A pointer that points to the end of the memory

Answer: b) A pointer that is not pointing to any memory location
Explanation:
A NULL pointer is one that does not point to any valid memory address.

99. **What is the output of the following code?**

```
int main() {
    int a = 10, b = 20;
    int *ptr = &a;
    *ptr = 30;
    printf("%d %d", a, b);
    return 0;
}
```

- a) `10 20`
- b) `30 20`
- c) `10 30`
- d) `30 30`

Answer: b) 30 20
Explanation:
The pointer ptr points to a. Modifying *ptr changes the value of a to 30. The value of b remains unchanged.

100. **What is the result of the following expression: `3 & 5`?**
   - a) `1`
   - b) `3`
   - c) `5`

- d) `7`

Answer: a) 1

Explanation:

The & operator is the bitwise AND operator.

Binary for 3: 0011

Binary for 5: 0101

0011 & 0101 = 0001, which is 1.

101. **Which of the following is not a valid C preprocessor directive?**
    - a) `#include`
    - b) `#define`
    - c) `#undef`
    - d) `#import`

    Answer: d) #import
    Explanation:
    #import is not a valid preprocessor directive in C. It is used in Objective-C.

102. **What will be the output of the following code?**

```
#include <stdio.h>
int main() {
   int arr[] = {1, 2, 3, 4, 5};
   int *ptr = arr + 2;
   printf("%d", *ptr);
   return 0;
}
```

- a) `1`
- b) `2`
- c) `3`
- d) `4`

Answer: c) 3

Explanation:
The pointer ptr points to the third element of the array (arr[2]), which has the value 3.

103. **Which of the following is true about `sizeof` operator in C?**
    - a) It returns the size of the data type in bits
    - b) It returns the size of the data type in bytes
    - c) It can be used only with primitive data types
    - d) It cannot be used with arrays

    Answer: b) It returns the size of the data type in bytes
    Explanation:
    The sizeof operator returns the size of a data type or object in bytes.

104. **What is the output of the following code?**

```
#include <stdio.h>
void fun(int x) {
    x = x + 10;
}
int main() {
    int a = 5;
    fun(a);
    printf("%d", a);
    return 0;
}
```

    - a) `5`
    - b) `10`
    - c) `15`
    - d) `0`

    Answer: a) 5
    Explanation:
    The function fun() modifies a local copy of a, so the value of

a in main() remains unchanged.

105. Which function is used to open a file for reading in binary mode in C?
- a) `fopen("filename", "rb")`
- b) `fopen("filename", "r")`
- c) `open("filename", "r")`
- d) `open("filename", "rb")`

Answer: a) fopen("filename", "rb")
Explanation:
The mode "rb" is used to open a file for reading in binary mode.

106. What will be the output of the following code?

```
#include <stdio.h>
int main() {
    int x = 5;
    printf("%d", x++ + ++x);
    return 0;
}
```

- a) `10`
- b) `11`
- c) `12`
- d) Undefined behavior

Answer: d) Undefined behavior
Explanation:
The expression modifies x multiple times without a sequence point, leading to undefined behavior.

107. Which of the following is a valid function declaration in C?
- a) `int func(int x);`

- b) `func(int x);`
- c) `function func(int x);`
- d) `int func(x);`

Answer: a) int func(int x);
Explanation:
A valid function declaration specifies the return type, function name, and parameter types. The other options have syntax errors.

108. **What is the result of the expression `0 && 1` in C?**
    - a) `0`
    - b) `1`
    - c) `True`
    - d) `False`

    Answer: a) 0
    Explanation:
    The logical AND (&&) operator evaluates to 0 (false) if any operand is 0.

109. **Which of the following is used to terminate a loop in C?**
    - a) `continue`
    - b) `break`
    - c) `exit`
    - d) `return`

    Answer: b) break

    Explanation:

    The break statement exits a loop prematurely.

    continue skips to the next iteration.

    exit terminates the program.

    return exits the current function.

SUBJECTIVE QUESTION AND ANSWER

1. Explain the basic structure of a C program with an example.

Answer:

The basic structure of a C program includes the following components:

1. **Preprocessor Directives**: Instructions to include libraries, e.g., #include<stdio.h>.
2. **Main Function**: The entry point of the program, defined as int main().
3. **Variable Declarations**: Declaration of variables used in the program.
4. **Executable Statements**: The logic or functionality of the program, enclosed within {} of the main() function.
5. **Return Statement**: Typically return 0;, which indicates successful program execution.

Example:

```
#include<stdio.h> // Preprocessor Directive

int main() {    // Main Function
   int a, b, sum; // Variable Declarations
   a = 10;    // Assign values
   b = 20;
   sum = a + b; // Perform addition
```

```
    printf("Sum = %d", sum); // Output
    return 0;    // Return statement
}
```

OUTPUT
Sum = 30

Here's a step-by-step explanation of the code:

```
#include<stdio.h> // Preprocessor Directive
```

- **#include<stdio.h>**: This is a preprocessor directive that tells the compiler to include the Standard Input Output (I/O) library, stdio.h. This library allows the use of input/output functions, such as printf() for displaying output to the screen.

```
int main() {    // Main Function
```

- **int main()**: This is the main function where the program starts executing. In C, the program execution begins from the main() function. The int before main indicates that the function will return an integer value to the operating system at the end of its execution.

```
int a, b, sum; // Variable Declarations
```

- **int a, b, sum;**: This line declares three integer variables (a, b, and sum). These variables are used to store integer values. In this case, a and b will store the numbers we want to add, and sum will store the result of their addition.

```
a = 10;    // Assign values
b = 20;
```

- **a = 10; and b = 20;**: Here, we are assigning the values 10 and 20 to the variables a and b, respectively. These are the values that we will add.

```
sum = a + b;  // Perform addition
```

- **sum = a + b;:** This line adds the values of a and b, and stores the result in the sum variable. In this case, 10 + 20 is calculated, and the result (30) is stored in sum.

```
printf("Sum = %d", sum); // Output
```

- **printf("Sum = %d", sum);:** This line prints the value of sum to the console. The %d is a format specifier that tells printf to print an integer value. It will print the value stored in the sum variable. In this case, it will print Sum = 30.

```
   return 0;    // Return statement
}
```

return 0;: This is the return statement of the main function. The 0 indicates that the program has executed successfully. It returns this value to the operating system when the program finishes.

Overall Execution:

1. The program starts and includes the necessary I/O library.
2. The main function begins execution, declaring and initializing the variables a, b, and sum.
3. It performs the addition a + b and stores the result in sum.
4. The printf function displays the result (Sum = 30) on the screen.
5. The program ends and returns 0 to indicate successful execution.

2. What are the primary data types in C? Explain with

examples.

Answer:

C has the following primary data types:

1. **Integer (int):** Used for whole numbers. Example:

```
int age = 20;
```

2. **Float (float):** Used for decimal values. Example:

```
float pi = 3.14;
```

3. **Character (char):** Used for single characters. Example:

```
char grade = 'A';
```

4. **Void (void):** Represents no value or type. Example:

```
void functionName();
```

---

3. Write a C program to find the largest of three numbers using if-else statements.

Answer:

```
#include<stdio.h>

int main() {
    int num1, num2, num3, largest;

    printf("Enter three numbers: ");
    scanf("%d %d %d", &num1, &num2, &num3);

    if (num1 > num2 && num1 > num3) {
        largest = num1;
    } else if (num2 > num3) {
        largest = num2;
    } else {
        largest = num3;
```

```
    }
    printf("The largest number is: %d", largest);
    return 0;
}
```

OUTPUT
Enter three numbers: 99 98 100
The largest number is: 100

Explanation:

1. Preprocessor Directive:

```
#include<stdio.h>
```

- This includes the standard input/output header file (stdio.h) which contains the functions printf() and scanf(). These are used for printing output and taking input respectively.

2. Main Function:

```
int main() {
```

- This is the entry point of the program where execution begins.

3. Variable Declaration:

```
int num1, num2, num3, largest;
```

- Here, four integer variables are declared:
    - num1, num2, and num3 will store the three numbers entered by the user.
    - largest will store the largest number out of the three.

4. Prompting for User Input:

```
printf("Enter three numbers: ");
```

- This prints the message "Enter three numbers: "

to the console, prompting the user to input three numbers.

5. **Taking User Input**:

```
scanf("%d %d %d", &num1, &num2, &num3);
```

- scanf() is used to read three integers entered by the user. These values are stored in num1, num2, and num3.

6. **Finding the Largest Number**:

```
if (num1 > num2 && num1 > num3) {
    largest = num1;
} else if (num2 > num3) {
    largest = num2;
} else {
    largest = num3;
}
```

- The if-else block checks which of the three numbers is the largest:
  - **First condition**: If num1 is greater than both num2 and num3, then num1 is the largest, and largest is set to num1.
  - **Second condition**: If the first condition is false (i.e., num1 is not the largest), it checks whether num2 is greater than num3. If true, num2 becomes the largest.
  - **Else**: If neither of the first two conditions is true, it means num3 is the largest, so largest is set to num3.

7. **Displaying the Result**:

```
printf("The largest number is: %d", largest);
```

- This prints the largest number using printf() and the value stored in the largest variable.

8. **End of the Program**:

```
return 0;
```

- This statement indicates the end of the main() function. Returning 0 signals successful execution of the program.

---

4. What are the different types of user-defined functions in C? Explain with examples.

Answer:

User-defined functions in C can be classified into four types:

1. **Function with no arguments and no return value**: Example:

```
void greet() {
    printf("Hello, World!");
}
```

void: This indicates that the function does not return any value. In other words, it performs an action but doesn't provide any output to the caller.

greet(): This is the name of the function. It has no parameters (i.e., the empty parentheses ()), meaning it does not take any input from the caller when invoked.

2. **Function with arguments but no return value**: Example:

```
void greet(char name[]) {
    printf("Hello, %s", name);
}
```

void: The return type of the function is void, meaning it does not return any value.

greet: The name of the function is greet.

char name[]: The parameter name[] is an array of characters. It is used to store a string (a sequence of characters). In C, strings are terminated by a null character

(\0) at the end.

3. **Function with no arguments but a return value**: Example:

```
int getNumber() {
    return 10;
}
```

int: This specifies the return type of the function. In this case, the function will return an integer (whole number).

getNumber: This is the name of the function. You can call this function by this name to invoke its behavior.

(): These parentheses indicate that the function does not take any arguments (i.e., it does not require any input when called).

4. **Function with arguments and a return value**: Example:

```
int add(int a, int b) {
    return a + b;
}
```

int: This specifies the return type of the function, which means that this function will return an integer value.

add: This is the name of the function. It indicates that the function is responsible for performing an addition operation.

(int a, int b): These are the parameters of the function. The function takes two integer arguments, a and b, which represent the values that will be added together.

---

5. Write a program to find the sum of elements in an array.
Answer:

```
#include<stdio.h>

int main() {
    int arr[5], i, sum = 0;

    printf("Enter 5 integers: ");
```

```
        for (i = 0; i < 5; i++) {
    scanf("%d", &arr[i]);
    sum += arr[i];
    }

    printf("The sum of the elements is: %d", sum);
    return 0;
}
```

OUTPUT
Enter 5 integers: 2 3 6 8 1
The sum of the elements is: 20

This C program calculates the sum of five integers entered by the user. Let's break it down step by step:

1. Header File Inclusion

```
#include <stdio.h>
```

- The #include <stdio.h> line includes the standard input/output library, which is necessary for functions like printf() (to print output) and scanf() (to read input from the user).

2. Main Function Declaration

```
int main() {
```

- The main() function is the entry point of every C program. It is where the program starts execution.

3. Variable Declaration

```
int arr[5], i, sum = 0;
```

- arr[5]: Declares an integer array arr of size 5 to store the five integers that the user will input.
- i: A variable used as a loop counter in the for loop.
- sum = 0: Initializes a variable sum to 0, which will be

used to accumulate the sum of the integers.

4. Prompt User for Input

```
printf("Enter 5 integers: ");
```

- printf() is used to display a message asking the user to enter 5 integers.

5. Reading User Input

```
for (i = 0; i < 5; i++) {
   scanf("%d", &arr[i]);
   sum += arr[i];
}
```

- This for loop iterates 5 times (from i = 0 to i = 4), allowing the user to input 5 integers.
- Inside the loop:
    - scanf("%d", &arr[i]): Reads an integer from the user and stores it in the i-th index of the array arr.
    - sum += arr[i]: Adds the integer stored in arr[i] to sum, accumulating the sum of the integers entered so far.

6. Displaying the Sum

```
printf("The sum of the elements is: %d", sum);
```

- After the loop ends, the printf() function is used to display the final value of sum, which is the total sum of the five integers entered by the user.

7. Return Statement

```
return 0;
```

- The return 0; statement indicates that the program has completed successfully. In C, a return value of 0 from main() typically signifies successful execution.

6. Explain the relationship between arrays and pointers in C.

Answer:

In C, arrays and pointers are closely related because:

1. **Base Address**: The name of an array represents its base address. For example, if int arr[5] is defined, arr points to the address of the first element arr[0].
2. **Pointer Arithmetic**: You can use pointers to traverse an array. Example:

```
int arr[3] = {10, 20, 30};
int *ptr = arr;

for (int i = 0; i < 3; i++) {
    printf("%d ", *(ptr + i)); // Access array elements using pointers
}
```

OUTPUT
10 20 30

This code demonstrates accessing array elements using pointers in C. Let's break it down step by step:

1. Array Initialization:

```
int arr[3] = {10, 20, 30};
```

- An integer array arr of size 3 is created and initialized with values: 10, 20, and 30.
- This means that:
    - arr[0] = 10
    - arr[1] = 20
    - arr[2] = 30

2. Pointer Initialization:

```
int *ptr = arr;
```

- A pointer ptr of type int* is declared and initialized to point to the first element of the array arr.
- In C, the name of the array (arr) can be used as a pointer to its first element. Therefore, ptr now points to arr[0].

3. Loop:

```
for (int i = 0; i < 3; i++) {
   printf("%d ", *(ptr + i)); // Access array elements using pointers
}
```

- A for loop runs 3 times, starting from i = 0 to i = 2. The loop will print the values of the array elements, accessed using the pointer ptr.

4. Pointer Arithmetic in printf:

```
*(ptr + i)
```

- Inside the loop, *(ptr + i) is used to access array elements using pointer arithmetic.
    - The expression ptr + i moves the pointer ptr by i elements ahead in the array. For example:
        - When i = 0, ptr + 0 is the same as ptr (pointing to arr[0]).
        - When i = 1, ptr + 1 points to the second element of the array arr[1].
        - When i = 2, ptr + 2 points to the third element arr[2].
    - The * operator is then used to dereference the pointer, i.e., to access the value at the memory address pointed to by (ptr + i).

---

7. Write a program to read from a file and display its content.

Answer:

```c
#include<stdio.h>

int main() {
    FILE *file;
    char ch;

    file = fopen("example.txt", "r"); // Open file in read mode
    if (file == NULL) {
        printf("File not found!");
        return 1;
    }

    while ((ch = fgetc(file)) != EOF) {
        printf("%c", ch); // Display file content
    }

    fclose(file); // Close file
    return 0;
}
```

Here's a step-by-step explanation of the provided C code:

1. Include Standard Input/Output Library

```c
#include<stdio.h>
```

This line includes the standard input/output library (stdio.h) which allows the program to use functions like fopen, fgetc, printf, and fclose for file operations and displaying output to the console.

2. Main Function

```c
int main() {
```

The program execution starts from the main function. It's the entry point of a C program.

3. Declare Variables

```c
FILE *file;
char ch;
```

- FILE *file;: A pointer of type FILE is declared, which will be used to reference the file for reading.
- char ch;: A variable ch of type char is declared to store each character read from the file.

4. Open the File

```
file = fopen("example.txt", "r");
```

This line opens the file named example.txt in **read mode** ("r"). The fopen function returns a file pointer if the file is opened successfully or NULL if the file cannot be found or opened. The returned pointer is stored in the file variable.

5. Check for File Opening Error

```
if (file == NULL) {
    printf("File not found!");
    return 1;
}
```

- This block checks whether the file pointer is NULL, which indicates that the file could not be opened (e.g., if the file doesn't exist).
- If the file is not found, it prints the message "File not found!" and returns 1, terminating the program with an error code.

6. Read and Display File Content

```
while ((ch = fgetc(file)) != EOF) {
    printf("%c", ch);
}
```

- fgetc(file) is used to read one character at a time from the file. It returns the character as an integer.
- This loop continues until the end of the file is reached, which is denoted by EOF (End Of File).

- Inside the loop, the character is printed to the console using printf("%c", ch);.

7. Close the File

```
fclose(file);
```

- After reading the entire content, the file is closed using fclose(file). This releases any resources associated with the file and ensures that any changes (if writing was involved) are properly saved.

8. Return Statement

```
return 0;
```

- The main function returns 0, indicating successful execution of the program.

---

8. Explain dynamic memory allocation in C. Write a program to dynamically allocate memory for an array.

Answer:

Dynamic memory allocation in C allows for allocating memory during runtime using functions from the stdlib.h library, such as:

1. **malloc**: Allocates uninitialized memory.
2. **calloc**: Allocates memory initialized to zero.
3. **realloc**: Resizes allocated memory.
4. **free**: Frees allocated memory.

Program:

```
#include<stdio.h>
#include<stdlib.h> // Required for malloc, calloc, free

int main() {
    int *arr, n, i;
```

```
    printf("Enter the number of elements: ");
    scanf("%d", &n);

    arr = (int *)malloc(n * sizeof(int)); // Dynamic memory
allocation using malloc
    if (arr == NULL) {
        printf("Memory allocation failed!");
        return 1;
    }

    printf("Enter %d elements: ", n);
    for (i = 0; i < n; i++) {
        scanf("%d", &arr[i]);
    }

    printf("You entered: ");
    for (i = 0; i < n; i++) {
        printf("%d ", arr[i]);
    }

    free(arr); // Free allocated memory
    return 0;
}
```

OUTPUT
Enter the number of elements: 5
Enter 5 elements: 1
2
3
4
5
You entered: 1 2 3 4 5

Let's go through the code step by step:

1. Header Files:

```
#include<stdio.h>
#include<stdlib.h> // Required for malloc, calloc, free
```

- stdio.h: This header file is included to use input/output functions like printf and scanf.
- stdlib.h: This header file is included to use dynamic memory allocation functions like malloc, calloc, and free.

2. Main Function:

```
int main() {
    int *arr, n, i;
```

- The main() function is the entry point of the program.
- arr is a pointer to an integer, which will be used to store the dynamically allocated array.
- n is an integer variable to store the number of elements that the user wants to enter.
- i is an integer used for looping through the array.

3. Asking for the Number of Elements:

```
printf("Enter the number of elements: ");
    scanf("%d", &n);
```

printf: Prompts the user to enter the number of elements.
- scanf: Reads the number entered by the user and stores it in the variable n.

4. Dynamic Memory Allocation:

```
arr = (int *)malloc(n * sizeof(int)); // Dynamic memory allocation using malloc
```

- malloc(n * sizeof(int)): This function allocates memory for an array of n integers. The sizeof(int) gives the size of one integer in bytes, and multiplying it by n gives the total number of bytes needed.

- (int *): This is a typecast to convert the malloc return value (a void *) into an integer pointer (int *), so it can be used to store integer values.
- arr: Points to the beginning of the dynamically allocated memory block.

5. Checking Memory Allocation:

```
if (arr == NULL) {
    printf("Memory allocation failed!");
    return 1;
}
```

- if (arr == NULL): Checks whether memory allocation failed (if malloc returns NULL, the allocation was unsuccessful).
- printf: If memory allocation fails, an error message is displayed.
- return 1: Exits the program with an error code 1.

6. Taking Array Input from the User:

```
printf("Enter %d elements: ", n);
    for (i = 0; i < n; i++) {
        scanf("%d", &arr[i]);
    }
```

printf: Prompts the user to enter the n elements.
- The for loop iterates from i = 0 to i = n-1, allowing the user to input n integers.
- scanf("%d", &arr[i]): Reads an integer and stores it in the i-th index of the dynamically allocated array.

7. Displaying the Entered Elements:

```
printf("You entered: ");
for (i = 0; i < n; i++) {
    printf("%d ", arr[i]);
```

```
}
```

- printf: Displays the message "You entered: ".
- The second for loop iterates through the array and prints each element stored at arr[i].

8. Freeing Allocated Memory:

```
free(arr); // Free allocated memory
```

free(arr): This function deallocates the memory previously allocated using malloc. It's important to free dynamically allocated memory to avoid memory leaks.

9. Return Statement:

```
    return 0;
}
```

- return 0: Signals that the program has executed successfully and ends the main function.

Summary of Program Flow:
1. The user is prompted to enter the number of elements they want in an array.
2. Dynamic memory is allocated for the array using malloc.
3. The user enters the elements of the array.
4. The program displays the entered elements.
5. The allocated memory is freed using free to avoid memory leaks.
6. The program terminates.

---

9. What is recursion? Write a program to find the factorial of a number using recursion.
Answer:
Recursion is a process where a function calls itself to solve a

smaller instance of the problem until it reaches a base case. It is commonly used in problems like factorial, Fibonacci series, and tree traversal.

Program:

```c
#include<stdio.h>

int factorial(int n) {
   if (n == 0 || n == 1) { // Base case
      return 1;
   }
   return n * factorial(n - 1); // Recursive call
}

int main() {
   int num;
   printf("Enter a number: ");
   scanf("%d", &num);

   printf("Factorial of %d is %d", num, factorial(num));
   return 0;
}
```

OUTPUT
Enter a number: 5
Factorial of 5 is 120

#include<stdio.h>

This line includes the standard input/output library in C, which is necessary to use functions like printf() and scanf().

int factorial(int n) { ... }

This is the definition of a recursive function factorial(), which calculates the factorial of a given number n.

if (n == 0 || n == 1) { return 1; }

This is the **base case** for the recursion. A factorial of 0 or 1 is defined as 1. So, if the value of n is 0 or 1, the function will return 1 and stop further recursive calls. This prevents an infinite loop of recursion.

return n * factorial(n - 1);

This is the **recursive case**. If n is greater than 1, the function returns the result of multiplying n with the result of factorial(n - 1). This calls the factorial() function again with a decremented value of n. The recursion continues until the base case (n == 1) is reached.

For example:

- If n = 5, the function calculates 5 * factorial(4).
- factorial(4) calculates 4 * factorial(3), and so on, until factorial(1) returns 1.

int main() { ... }

This is the main() function where the program starts executing.

int num;

This declares an integer variable num, which will store the number entered by the user for which we want to calculate the factorial.

printf("Enter a number: ");

This prints the prompt to the user, asking them to enter a number.

scanf("%d", &num);

This line reads the number input by the user from the console and stores it in the variable num.

printf("Factorial of %d is %d", num, factorial(num));

This line prints the result. It calls the factorial() function with the value of num and prints the calculated factorial along with the input number. The %d format specifiers are used to print integers (the input number and the result of the factorial function).

return 0;

This returns 0 from the main() function, signaling that the program has executed successfully. This is the standard way to indicate successful execution in C.

Example Execution:

If the user inputs 5, the program will calculate the factorial as:

```
factorial(5) = 5 * factorial(4)
factorial(4) = 4 * factorial(3)
factorial(3) = 3 * factorial(2)
factorial(2) = 2 * factorial(1)
factorial(1) = 1 (base case)
```

---

10. Describe the storage classes in C with examples.

Answer:

Storage classes in C determine the **scope, lifetime, and visibility** of variables. The four storage classes are:

1. **auto**: Default for local variables.

```
void func() {
    auto int x = 10;
}
```

void func()
- This line defines a function named func with no return type (void means it doesn't return anything).
- The function doesn't take any parameters, as the parentheses are empty.

auto int x = 10;

This line is a variable declaration inside the function. It contains the following components:

- **auto**: This keyword is used to let the compiler deduce the type of the variable. The type is determined based on the initializer (in this case, 10), so x will be of type int because 10 is an integer.
- **int**: Normally, auto is used alone to let the compiler decide the type. However, in this case, it is combined with int, which is redundant. This is not incorrect but unnecessary and unusual. The keyword auto alone would suffice to infer the type.
- **x**: This is the variable name. It will hold the value

assigned to it, which in this case is 10.

- **= 10**: This initializes the variable x with the value 10. Since auto will infer the type of x as int, x will be an integer with the value 10.

2. **register**: Requests to store the variable in CPU registers for faster access.

```
void func() {
    register int counter = 0;
}
```

1. **Function Declaration**:

```
void func()
```

- This line defines a function named func that doesn't return any value (indicated by void).
- The function doesn't take any parameters.

2. **Variable Declaration**:

```
register int counter = 0;
```

- **register**: This is a storage class specifier. It suggests to the compiler that the variable counter should be stored in a CPU register, if possible, for faster access. It's a hint to the compiler, but the compiler may ignore it if it determines that the variable cannot be stored in a register.
  - **Note**: You cannot take the address of a variable declared with register (i.e., no &counter).
- **int**: This specifies the data type of the variable. In this case, counter is of type int, meaning it will store integer values.
- **counter**: This is the name of the variable being declared.

◦ **= 0**: This initializes the variable counter with the value 0.

Summary of the code:

- The function func() defines a local variable counter of type int that is suggested to be stored in a CPU register for faster access, and it is initialized to 0.

3. **static**: Retains the value of a variable between function calls.

```
void func() {
   static int count = 0;
   count++;
   printf("%d", count);
}
```

1. **Function Declaration:**

```
void func()
```

This line declares a function named func that takes no parameters and returns no value (void).

2. **Static Variable Declaration:**

```
static int count = 0;
```

Inside the function, we declare a variable count of type int and initialize it to 0. The key aspect here is the use of the static keyword.

   ◦ **Static Keyword:** Normally, when a variable is declared inside a function, it is created each time the function is called, and it is destroyed when the function exits. However, a static variable persists its value between function calls. This means that even after the function func() returns, the value of count remains in memory and is not reinitialized to 0 the next time func() is called.

- So, the first time the function is called, count is initialized to 0. On subsequent calls, count will retain its previous value.

3. **Incrementing the Count:**

```
count++;
```

This line increments the count variable by 1. Every time func() is called, the value of count is increased by 1, starting from 0. If the function has been called before, it will continue from the last incremented value.

4. **Printing the Count:**

```
printf("%d", count);
```

This line uses the printf function to print the value of count to the console. The %d format specifier is used to print an integer.

Example:

- **First call to func():**
    - count is initialized to 0 (because it's static).
    - count is incremented to 1.
    - The value 1 is printed.
- **Second call to func():**
    - count retains the value from the previous call, which was 1.
    - count is incremented to 2.
    - The value 2 is printed.
- **Third call to func():**
    - count retains the value from the previous call, which was 2.
    - count is incremented to 3.
    - The value 3 is printed.

In summary, the static variable count keeps its value across multiple calls to func(), so it keeps counting how many times the function has been called.

4. **extern**: Declares a global variable accessible across multiple files.

   | extern int x; // Declared in another file |

extern Keyword:

- The extern keyword is used to declare a variable that is defined in another source file or translation unit. It tells the compiler that the variable x exists somewhere, but it does not define it in the current file.
- This helps in sharing variables between different files in a program.

---

11. Write a program to reverse a string without using built-in functions.

Answer:

```
#include<stdio.h>
#include<string.h>

void reverseString(char str[]) {
    int start = 0, end = strlen(str) - 1;
    char temp;

    while (start < end) {
        temp = str[start];
        str[start] = str[end];
        str[end] = temp;
        start++;
        end--;
    }
}

int main() {
    char str[100];
    printf("Enter a string: ");
```

```c
    scanf("%s", str);

    reverseString(str);
    printf("Reversed string: %s", str);

    return 0;
}
```

OUTPUT
Enter a string: hello
Reversed string: olleh

This C program reverses a string entered by the user. Let's go through the code step by step:

1. Include Header Files:

```c
#include<stdio.h>
#include<string.h>
```

- stdio.h is included for input/output functions like printf and scanf.
- string.h is included to use string-related functions like strlen.

2. Function Definition:

```c
void reverseString(char str[]) {
    int start = 0, end = strlen(str) - 1;
    char temp;

    while (start < end) {
        temp = str[start];
        str[start] = str[end];
        str[end] = temp;
        start++;
        end--;
    }
}
```

- reverseString is a function that reverses the string

passed as a parameter (str[]).
- **Parameters:**
  - char str[]: A character array (string) passed to the function.
- **Local Variables:**
  - int start = 0: The index of the first character of the string.
  - int end = strlen(str) - 1: The index of the last character of the string (since strlen(str) gives the length of the string, and indexing starts from 0).
  - char temp: A temporary variable used to swap characters.
- **While Loop:**
  - while (start < end) keeps running as long as the start index is less than the end index.
  - Inside the loop, characters from the start and end positions are swapped:
    - temp = str[start]: Store the character at the start index in temp.
    - str[start] = str[end]: Replace the character at the start index with the character at the end index.
    - str[end] = temp: Place the character from temp (originally at start) into the end position.
  - Then, start++ and end-- are used to move the start index forward and the end index backward, so the next characters will be swapped.

3. Main Function:

```
int main() {
    char str[100];
    printf("Enter a string: ");
    scanf("%s", str);
```

```
    reverseString(str);
    printf("Reversed string: %s", str);

    return 0;
}
```

- char str[100]: A character array str is declared with a maximum size of 100. It will hold the user input.
- printf("Enter a string: ");: Prompts the user to enter a string.
- scanf("%s", str);: Reads a string from the user and stores it in str. Note that scanf("%s", str) will only read input until the first space is encountered (so it doesn't handle multi-word input).
- reverseString(str);: Calls the reverseString function to reverse the string str.
- printf("Reversed string: %s", str);: Prints the reversed string.
- return 0;: Ends the main function and indicates successful program execution.

Example Walkthrough:

Let's say the input string is "hello".

- Initially: str = "hello", start = 0, end = 4 (length of "hello" - 1).
- 1st iteration of the loop:
    - temp = 'h', str[start] = 'o', str[end] = 'h'
    - str = "oellh", start = 1, end = 3.
- 2nd iteration of the loop:
    - temp = 'e', str[start] = 'l', str[end] = 'e'
    - str = "olleh", start = 2, end = 2 (now start equals end, so the loop stops).
- Final output: "Reversed string: olleh".

Summary:

- The program takes a string input, reverses it using a function, and prints the reversed string.
- The reverseString function uses a two-pointer technique (start and end) to swap characters until the entire string is reversed.

---

12. Explain bitwise operators in C with examples. Write a program to count the number of set bits in an integer.

Answer:

Bitwise operators perform operations at the bit level. They include:

1. &: AND
2. |: OR
3. ^: XOR
4. ~: NOT
5. <<: Left Shift
6. >>: Right Shift

Program to Count Set Bits:

```c
#include<stdio.h>

int countSetBits(int num) {
    int count = 0;
    while (num > 0) {
        count += num & 1; // Check the least significant bit
        num >>= 1;    // Right shift the number
    }
    return count;
}

int main() {
    int num;
    printf("Enter an integer: ");
```

```
    scanf("%d", &num);

    printf("Number of set bits: %d", countSetBits(num));
    return 0;
}
```

OUTPUT
Enter an integer: 29
Number of set bits: 4

The provided C code counts the number of set bits (1s) in the binary representation of an integer. Here's a step-by-step explanation:

1. Function Declaration:

```
int countSetBits(int num)
```

- The function countSetBits takes an integer num as input and returns the number of set bits (1s) in its binary representation.

2. Variable Initialization:

```
int count = 0;
```

- A local variable count is initialized to 0. This will be used to store the total number of set bits.

3. While Loop:

```
while (num > 0)
```

- The loop continues as long as num is greater than 0. It will repeatedly check each bit of the number until all bits are checked.

4. Counting the Set Bit:

```
count += num & 1;
```

- The expression num & 1 performs a bitwise AND operation between num and 1. This operation isolates

the least significant bit (LSB) of num.
  - If the LSB is 1 (set bit), the result of num & 1 will be 1.
  - If the LSB is 0, the result will be 0.
- The result is added to count, increasing the count of set bits if the LSB is 1.

5. Right Shifting the Number:

```
num >>= 1;
```

- This operation right-shifts num by one position, effectively discarding the least significant bit that was just checked.
- This allows the next iteration of the loop to check the next bit of the number.

6. Returning the Count:

```
return count;
```

- After the loop finishes (i.e., when num becomes 0), the total count of set bits is returned.

7. Main Function:

```c
int main() {
    int num;
    printf("Enter an integer: ");
    scanf("%d", &num);
    printf("Number of set bits: %d", countSetBits(num));
    return 0;
}
```

- **Input Prompt:** printf("Enter an integer: "); asks the user to enter an integer.
- **Input Reading:** scanf("%d", &num); reads the integer entered by the user and stores it in the variable num.

- **Calling the Function:** printf("Number of set bits: %d", countSetBits(num)); calls the countSetBits function and prints the result.
- **Program End:** return 0; indicates that the program finished successfully.

Example Walkthrough:

Let's consider the input num = 29.
- In binary, 29 is represented as 11101.
- The function would process the bits as follows:
  - num = 11101 → LSB is 1 → count = 1, right shift to 1110.
  - num = 1110 → LSB is 0 → count = 1, right shift to 111.
  - num = 111 → LSB is 1 → count = 2, right shift to 11.
  - num = 11 → LSB is 1 → count = 3, right shift to 1.
  - num = 1 → LSB is 1 → count = 4, right shift to 0.
- Now, num = 0, so the loop ends, and count = 4 is returned, indicating there are 4 set bits in the binary representation of 29.

---

13. Write a program to copy the content of one file to another in C.

Answer:

```
#include<stdio.h>

int main() {
   FILE *source, *dest;
   char sourceFile[100], destFile[100], ch;

   printf("Enter source file name: ");
   scanf("%s", sourceFile);
```

```
    printf("Enter destination file name: ");
    scanf("%s", destFile);

    source = fopen(sourceFile, "r");
    if (source == NULL) {
        printf("Source file not found!");
        return 1;
    }

    dest = fopen(destFile, "w");

    while ((ch = fgetc(source)) != EOF) {
        fputc(ch, dest);
    }

    printf("File copied successfully!");

    fclose(source);
    fclose(dest);
    return 0;
}
```

This program is designed to copy the contents of one file (source file) to another file (destination file). Here's a step-by-step explanation of the code:

1. Include header files

```
#include<stdio.h>
```

- This line includes the stdio.h header file, which contains functions for input and output operations like printf(), scanf(), fopen(), fgetc(), fputc(), and fclose().

2. Define main function

```
int main() {
```

- This is the entry point of the C program. The int

signifies that the function will return an integer value.

3. Declare file pointers and variables

```
FILE *source, *dest;
char sourceFile[100], destFile[100], ch;
```

- FILE *source, *dest;: Declares two file pointers. source is used to read the source file, and dest is used to write to the destination file.
- char sourceFile[100], destFile[100], ch;: Declares character arrays to store the filenames of the source and destination files, and a char variable ch to store individual characters read from the source file.

4. Prompt user for source and destination filenames

```
printf("Enter source file name: ");
scanf("%s", sourceFile);

printf("Enter destination file name: ");
scanf("%s", destFile);
```

- The program prompts the user to input the name of the source file and the destination file. The filenames are stored in the sourceFile and destFile arrays using scanf().

5. Open the source file

```
source = fopen(sourceFile, "r");
if (source == NULL) {
   printf("Source file not found!");
   return 1;
}
```

- fopen(sourceFile, "r") attempts to open the source file in **read mode** ("r").
  - If the file cannot be opened (for example, if the file does not exist), fopen() returns NULL.

- The if (source == NULL) condition checks if the file was successfully opened. If not, it prints an error message ("Source file not found!") and exits the program by returning 1.

6. Open the destination file

```
dest = fopen(destFile, "w");
```

- fopen(destFile, "w") opens the destination file in **write mode** ("w").
  - If the file doesn't exist, it is created. If it already exists, its content will be overwritten.

7. Copy content from source to destination

```
while ((ch = fgetc(source)) != EOF) {
    fputc(ch, dest);
}
```

- fgetc(source) reads one character at a time from the source file and stores it in the variable ch.
- The while loop continues reading characters until it reaches the **End of File** (EOF).
- fputc(ch, dest) writes the character stored in ch to the destination file.

8. Display success message

```
printf("File copied successfully!");
```

- After the loop finishes (i.e., when the entire file has been copied), the program prints "File copied successfully!".

9. Close the files

```
fclose(source);
fclose(dest);
```

- fclose(source) and fclose(dest) close the source and destination files, respectively. It's important to close files after finishing reading or writing to ensure proper resource management.

10. End of the program

```
return 0;
```

- The return 0; statement indicates that the program executed successfully and exits the main() function.

Summary:

- This program copies the content of one file (specified by the user) into another file, character by character.
- It handles file opening, reading, writing, and error checking (if the source file cannot be found).
- It assumes that the source and destination files are text files.

Example Run of the Program:

Case 1: When the source file exists

Input:

Enter source file name: source.txt

Enter destination file name: dest.txt

Process:

1. The program attempts to open source.txt in read mode. If successful, it continues.
2. It opens dest.txt in write mode (creates a new file if it doesn't exist).
3. It reads each character from source.txt and writes it to dest.txt.
4. After copying, the program prints a success message.

Output:

File copied successfully!

Files after execution:
- source.txt: Original file remains unchanged.
- dest.txt: Contains an exact copy of the content from source.txt.

Case 2: When the source file does not exist
Input:
Enter source file name: non_existing_file.txt
Enter destination file name: dest.txt
Process:
1. The program attempts to open non_existing_file.txt in read mode.
2. Since the file does not exist, fopen() returns NULL.
3. The program prints an error message and terminates.

Output:
Source file not found!

Case 3: Empty source file
Input:
Enter source file name: empty.txt
Enter destination file name: dest.txt
Process:
1. The program opens empty.txt successfully.
2. Reads the file content, which is empty (no characters to copy).
3. Writes nothing to dest.txt (file will be empty as well).
4. Prints success message.

Output:
File copied successfully!
Files after execution:
- empty.txt: Still empty.

- dest.txt: Also empty, but the program completed successfully.

Case 4: Overwriting destination file
Input:

Enter source file name: source.txt
Enter destination file name: dest.txt

Process:
1. The program opens source.txt successfully.
2. Opens dest.txt in write mode, which overwrites any existing content in dest.txt.
3. Copies the content from source.txt to dest.txt.

Output:

File copied successfully!

Files after execution:
- dest.txt: Contains the new content copied from source.txt. Any previous content in dest.txt is erased.

---

14. Write a program to perform matrix multiplication in C.

Answer:

```
#include<stdio.h>

int main() {
    int a[3][3], b[3][3], c[3][3] = {0};
    int i, j, k;

    printf("Enter elements of matrix A (3x3): ");
    for (i = 0; i < 3; i++) {
        for (j = 0; j < 3; j++) {
            scanf("%d", &a[i][j]);
        }
```

```c
        }

    printf("Enter elements of matrix B (3x3): ");
    for (i = 0; i < 3; i++) {
        for (j = 0; j < 3; j++) {
            scanf("%d", &b[i][j]);
        }
    }

    // Matrix multiplication
    for (i = 0; i < 3; i++) {
        for (j = 0; j < 3; j++) {
            for (k = 0; k < 3; k++) {
                c[i][j] += a[i][k] * b[k][j];
            }
        }
    }

    printf("Resultant matrix C:\n");
    for (i = 0; i < 3; i++) {
        for (j = 0; j < 3; j++) {
            printf("%d ", c[i][j]);
        }
        printf("\n");
    }

    return 0;
}
```

OUTPUT
Enter elements of matrix A (3x3):
1 2 3
4 5 6
7 8 9

Enter elements of matrix B (3x3):
9 8 7
6 5 4

3 2 1

Resultant matrix C:
30   24 18
84   69 54
138 114 90

The C program you've provided multiplies two 3x3 matrices, A and B, and stores the result in matrix C. Let's go through it step by step:

1. Variable Declaration

```
int a[3][3], b[3][3], c[3][3] = {0};
int i, j, k;
```

- **a[3][3]**: This is a 3x3 matrix to store the elements of matrix A.
- **b[3][3]**: This is a 3x3 matrix to store the elements of matrix B.
- **c[3][3] = {0}**: This is a 3x3 matrix to store the result of matrix multiplication. It's initialized to all zeroes.
- **i, j, k**: These are integer variables used for iteration in the loops.

2. Input for Matrix A

```
printf("Enter elements of matrix A (3x3): ");
for (i = 0; i < 3; i++) {
   for (j = 0; j < 3; j++) {
      scanf("%d", &a[i][j]);
   }
}
```

- The program prompts the user to enter the elements of matrix A.
- **scanf("%d", &a[i][j])** is used inside nested loops to fill the 3x3 matrix A with integers.

3. Input for Matrix B

```
printf("Enter elements of matrix B (3x3): ");
for (i = 0; i < 3; i++) {
   for (j = 0; j < 3; j++) {
      scanf("%d", &b[i][j]);
   }
}
```

- Similar to matrix A, the program prompts the user to enter the elements for matrix B and stores them in matrix B using nested loops.

4. Matrix Multiplication

```
for (i = 0; i < 3; i++) {
   for (j = 0; j < 3; j++) {
      for (k = 0; k < 3; k++) {
         c[i][j] += a[i][k] * b[k][j];
      }
   }
}
```

- The matrix multiplication process begins here.
- The outer two loops iterate over the rows of matrix A (denoted by i) and the columns of matrix B (denoted by j).
- The innermost loop iterates over the elements in the rows of A and columns of B (denoted by k), performing the necessary multiplication and addition.
    - **c[i][j] += a[i][k] * b[k][j];**: This calculates the element in the result matrix C by multiplying corresponding elements from matrix A and matrix B and adding them together.

5. Printing the Resultant Matrix

```
printf("Resultant matrix C:\n");
```

```c
for (i = 0; i < 3; i++) {
   for (j = 0; j < 3; j++) {
      printf("%d ", c[i][j]);
   }
   printf("\n");
}
```

- This loop prints the resultant matrix C.
- The outer loop iterates over the rows of matrix C, and the inner loop iterates over the columns of matrix C, printing each element.

6. Return Statement

```c
return 0;
```

- This line indicates the successful termination of the program and returns 0.

Summary of Matrix Multiplication:

Matrix multiplication follows the rule:

- If A is of size m×n and B is of size n×p, the resulting matrix C will have the dimensions m×p.
- For each element C[i][j], it is calculated as the sum of products:
  C[i][j] = A[i][0] * B[0][j] + A[i][1] * B[1][j] + ... + A[i][n-1] * B[n-1][j].

Since you're multiplying two 3x3 matrices, the multiplication will compute the sum of products for each element in the result matrix.

Let's walk through an example input and output for your matrix multiplication program.

Example Input:

Matrix A:

```
1 2 3
```

```
4 5 6
7 8 9
```

Matrix B:

```
9 8 7
6 5 4
3 2 1
```

Matrix Multiplication Process:

The resultant matrix C is calculated as follows:

1. For C[0][0]: C[0][0]=(1*9)+(2*6)+(3*3)=9+12+9=30
2. For C[0][1]: C[0][1]=(1*8)+(2*5)+(3*2)=8+10+6=24
3. For C[0][2]: C[0][2]=(1*7)+(2*4)+(3*1)=7+8+3=18
4. For C[1][0]: C[1][0]=(4*9)+(5*6)+(6*3)=36+30+18=84
5. For C[1][1]: C[1][1]=(4*8)+(5*5)+(6*2)=32+25+12=69
6. For C[1][2]: C[1][2]=(4*7)+(5*4)+(6*1)=28+20+6=54
7. For C[2][0]: C[2][0]=(7*9)+(8*6)+(9*3)=63+48+27=138
8. For C[2][1]: C[2][1]=(7*8)+(8*5)+(9*2)=56+40+18=114
9. For C[2][2]: C[2][2]=(7*7)+(8*4)+(9*1)=49+32+9=90

Resultant Matrix C:

```
30  24  18
84  69  54
138 114 90
```

CODING QUESTIONS

1. Reverse a String

Question: Write a C program to reverse a string.

Answer:

```c
#include <stdio.h>
#include <string.h>

void reverseString(char *str) {
    int n = strlen(str);
    for (int i = 0; i < n / 2; i++) {
        char temp = str[i];
        str[i] = str[n - i - 1];
        str[n - i - 1] = temp;
    }
}

int main() {
    char str[100];
    printf("Enter a string: ");
    fgets(str, sizeof(str), stdin);

    // Remove the newline character if present
    str[strcspn(str, "\n")] = '\0';

    reverseString(str);
    printf("Reversed string: %s\n", str);
    return 0;
}
```

OUTPUT
Enter a string: hello

> Reversed string: olleh

Let's go through the provided code step by step:

1. Header Files

```
#include <stdio.h>
#include <string.h>
```

- **#include <stdio.h>**: Allows the use of standard input/output functions like printf and gets.
- **#include <string.h>**: Includes string manipulation functions like strlen.

2. Function Declaration

```
void reverseString(char *str) {
    int n = strlen(str);
    for (int i = 0; i < n / 2; i++) {
        char temp = str[i];
        str[i] = str[n - i - 1];
        str[n - i - 1] = temp;
    }
}
```

Explanation:
- **Purpose**: Reverses the string passed to it.
- **int n = strlen(str);**
    - Determines the length of the string str.
    - n holds the number of characters in the string (excluding the null terminator \0).
- **Loop: for (int i = 0; i < n / 2; i++)**
    - Loops through the first half of the string.
    - Each iteration swaps the character at index i with the character at the corresponding position from the end (n - i - 1).

- **Swapping Logic**:

```
char temp = str[i];        // Save the current character to a temporary variable.
str[i] = str[n - i - 1];   // Replace it with the character from the other end.
str[n - i - 1] = temp;     // Copy the saved character to the other end.
```

  ◦ Ensures the string is reversed without losing any characters.

3. Main Function

```c
int main() {
   char str[100];
   printf("Enter a string: ");
   gets(str);
   reverseString(str);
   printf("Reversed string: %s\n", str);
   return 0;
}
```

Explanation:
1. **char str[100];**
   ◦ Declares a character array to store the string, with a maximum capacity of 99 characters (plus the null terminator).
2. **printf("Enter a string: ");**
   ◦ Prompts the user to enter a string.
3. **gets(str);**
   ◦ Reads the input string from the user.
   ◦ **Important Note**: gets is unsafe because it does not check for buffer overflows. It is recommended to use fgets instead.
4. **reverseString(str);**
   ◦ Calls the reverseString function to reverse the

input string.
   5. **printf("Reversed string: %s\n", str);**
      ◦ Prints the reversed string.
   6. **return 0;**
      ◦ Indicates that the program executed successfully.

2. Fibonacci Series

Question: Write a C program to generate the Fibonacci series up to n terms.

Answer:

```c
#include <stdio.h>

void fibonacci(int n) {
    int a = 0, b = 1, next;
    for (int i = 1; i <= n; i++) {
        printf("%d ", a);
        next = a + b;
        a = b;
        b = next;
    }
    printf("\n");
}

int main() {
    int n;
    printf("Enter the number of terms: ");
    scanf("%d", &n);
    fibonacci(n);
    return 0;
}
```

OUTPUT
Enter the number of terms: 5
0 1 1 2 3

Here is a step-by-step explanation of the given C program:

1. Headers

```
#include <stdio.h>
```

- The #include <stdio.h> directive includes the Standard Input/Output library, enabling functions like printf() and scanf().

2. Function Definition: fibonacci()

```
void fibonacci(int n) {
    int a = 0, b = 1, next;
    for (int i = 1; i <= n; i++) {
        printf("%d ", a);
        next = a + b;
        a = b;
        b = next;
    }
    printf("\n");
}
```

- **Purpose**: Prints the first n terms of the Fibonacci sequence.
- **Parameters**: Takes an integer n (number of terms to generate).
- **Local Variables**:
    - a: Tracks the current Fibonacci number (initially 0).
    - b: Tracks the next Fibonacci number (initially 1).
    - next: Temporary variable to calculate the next Fibonacci number.
- **Logic**:
    - A for loop iterates n times:

1. Print the current number a.
2. Calculate next as the sum of a and b.
3. Update a to the value of b (move to the next number).
4. Update b to the value of next.

3. Main Function

```
int main() {
   int n;
   printf("Enter the number of terms: ");
   scanf("%d", &n);
   fibonacci(n);
   return 0;
}
```

- **Steps:**
    1. Declare an integer variable n.
    2. Use printf() to ask the user to enter the number of terms.
    3. Use scanf() to read the user's input and store it in n.
    4. Call the fibonacci() function, passing n as an argument.
    5. Return 0 to indicate successful program execution.

4. Program Execution

- **Input:**
    - User enters the number of terms they want from the Fibonacci sequence, e.g., 5.
- **Output:**
    - The program prints the Fibonacci sequence up to the n terms.
- **Example Execution:**
    - Input: 5

- Output: 0 1 1 2 3

How the Fibonacci Sequence Works:
- Starts with 0 and 1.
- Each subsequent number is the sum of the previous two numbers.
- Example Sequence: 0, 1, 1, 2, 3, 5, 8, 13, ...

Example Walkthrough for Input n = 5:
1. **Initialization**:
    - a = 0, b = 1.
2. **Iteration**:
    - **1st iteration (i=1)**:
        - Print a → 0.
        - next = a + b = 0 + 1 = 1.
        - Update a = b = 1, b = next = 1.
    - **2nd iteration (i=2)**:
        - Print a → 1.
        - next = a + b = 1 + 1 = 2.
        - Update a = b = 1, b = next = 2.
    - **3rd iteration (i=3)**:
        - Print a → 1.
        - next = a + b = 1 + 2 = 3.
        - Update a = b = 2, b = next = 3.
    - **4th iteration (i=4)**:
        - Print a → 2.
        - next = a + b = 2 + 3 = 5.
        - Update a = b = 3, b = next = 5.
    - **5th iteration (i=5)**:
        - Print a → 3.
        - next = a + b = 3 + 5 = 8.
        - Update a = b = 5, b = next = 8.
3. **Output**: 0 1 1 2 3

Key Concepts:

- **Loop Iteration**: The for loop iterates exactly n times, ensuring the sequence is printed for the specified terms.

- **Fibonacci Logic**: The formula next = a + b and updates for a and b ensure the sequence progresses correctly.

3. Prime Number Check

Question: Write a C program to check if a given number is prime.
Answer:

```c
#include <stdio.h>

int isPrime(int n) {
    if (n <= 1) return 0;
    for (int i = 2; i <= n / 2; i++) {
        if (n % i == 0) return 0;
    }
    return 1;
}

int main() {
    int n;
    printf("Enter a number: ");
    scanf("%d", &n);
    if (isPrime(n)) {
        printf("%d is a prime number\n", n);
    } else {
        printf("%d is not a prime number\n", n);
    }
    return 0;
}
```

OUTPUT
Enter a number: 7
7 is a prime number

> Enter a number: 10
> 10 is not a prime number

This C program determines if a given number is a prime number or not. Here's a step-by-step explanation:

Code Breakdown

1. Header File Inclusion

```
#include <stdio.h>
```

- The program starts by including the stdio.h library, which is necessary for input/output functions like printf and scanf.

2. Function: isPrime

```
int isPrime(int n) {
   if (n <= 1) return 0;
   for (int i = 2; i <= n / 2; i++) {
      if (n % i == 0) return 0;
   }
   return 1;
}
```

- **Input:** An integer n.
- **Purpose:** Determines if the number n is prime.
- **Steps:**
  1. **Check if n is less than or equal to 1:**

```
if (n <= 1) return 0;
```

  - Numbers less than or equal to 1 are not prime. Return 0 (false).

  2. **Iterate from 2 to n / 2:**

```
for (int i = 2; i <= n / 2; i++) {
```

- Check divisors from 2 to n/2. If n is divisible by any of these, it is not prime.

3. **Check divisibility:**

```
if (n % i == 0) return 0;
```

- If n is divisible by i, return 0 (false), indicating n is not prime.

4. **Return 1 if no divisors are found:**

```
return 1;
```

- If the loop completes without finding a divisor, n is prime.

3. **Main Function**

```
int main() {
   int n;
   printf("Enter a number: ");
   scanf("%d", &n);
   if (isPrime(n)) {
      printf("%d is a prime number\n", n);
   } else {
      printf("%d is not a prime number\n", n);
   }
   return 0;
}
```

- **Steps:**
    1. **Declare a variable n:**

```
int n;
```

- Holds the user-provided input.

2. **Prompt the user for input:**

```
printf("Enter a number: ");
```

- Display a message asking the user to input a number.

3. **Read the input:**

```
scanf("%d", &n);
```

- Use scanf to read the input number from the user and store it in n.

4. **Check if n is prime:**

```
if (isPrime(n)) {
    printf("%d is a prime number\n", n);
} else {
    printf("%d is not a prime number\n", n);
}
```

- Call the isPrime function with n as the argument.
- If the function returns 1, print that the number is prime.
- Otherwise, print that it is not prime.

5. **Exit the program:**

```
return 0;
```

- Return 0 to indicate successful program termination.

How it Works

1. The program prompts the user to input a number.
2. It checks if the number is greater than 1.
3. If greater than 1, it checks for divisors from 2 to n/2.

4. If a divisor is found, the number is not prime. Otherwise, it is prime.
   5. The result is displayed to the user.

Example Execution

Input:

Enter a number: 7

Steps:

   1. isPrime(7) is called.
   2. 7 > 1 → proceed.
   3. Loop: i = 2 to 7 / 2 = 3.
      - 7 % 2 != 0
      - 7 % 3 != 0
   4. No divisors are found. isPrime(7) returns 1.
   5. Output: 7 is a prime number

Input:

Enter a number: 10

Steps:

   1. isPrime(10) is called.
   2. 10 > 1 → proceed.
   3. Loop: i = 2 to 10 / 2 = 5.
      - 10 % 2 == 0 → divisor found.
   4. isPrime(10) returns 0.
   5. Output: 10 is not a prime number

4. Factorial of a Number

Question: Write a C program to calculate the factorial of a number using recursion.

Answer:

```
#include<stdio.h>

int factorial(int n) {
```

```
    if (n == 0 || n == 1) { // Base case
       return 1;
    }
    return n * factorial(n - 1); // Recursive call
}
int main() {
    int num;
    printf("Enter a number: ");
    scanf("%d", &num);

    printf("Factorial of %d is %d", num, factorial(num));
    return 0;
}
```

OUTPUT
Enter a number: 5
Factorial of 5 is 120

#include<stdio.h>

This line includes the standard input/output library in C, which is necessary to use functions like printf() and scanf().

int factorial(int n) { ... }

This is the definition of a recursive function factorial(), which calculates the factorial of a given number n.

if (n == 0 || n == 1) { return 1; }

This is the **base case** for the recursion. A factorial of 0 or 1 is defined as 1. So, if the value of n is 0 or 1, the function will return 1 and stop further recursive calls. This prevents an infinite loop of recursion.

return n * factorial(n - 1);

This is the **recursive case**. If n is greater than 1, the function returns the result of multiplying n with the result of factorial(n - 1). This calls the factorial() function again with a decremented value of n. The recursion continues until the base case (n == 1) is reached.

For example:

- If n = 5, the function calculates 5 * factorial(4).
- factorial(4) calculates 4 * factorial(3), and so on, until factorial(1) returns 1.

int main() { ... }

This is the main() function where the program starts executing.

int num;

This declares an integer variable num, which will store the number entered by the user for which we want to calculate the factorial.

printf("Enter a number: ");

This prints the prompt to the user, asking them to enter a number.

scanf("%d", &num);

This line reads the number input by the user from the console and stores it in the variable num.

printf("Factorial of %d is %d", num, factorial(num));

This line prints the result. It calls the factorial() function with the value of num and prints the calculated factorial along with the input number. The %d format specifiers are used to print integers (the input number and the result of the factorial function).

return 0;

This returns 0 from the main() function, signaling that the program has executed successfully. This is the standard way to indicate successful execution in C.

Example Execution:

If the user inputs 5, the program will calculate the factorial as:

```
factorial(5) = 5 * factorial(4)
factorial(4) = 4 * factorial(3)
factorial(3) = 3 * factorial(2)
factorial(2) = 2 * factorial(1)
factorial(1) = 1 (base case)
```

5. Binary Search

Question: Write a C program to implement binary search on a sorted array.

Answer:

```c
#include <stdio.h>

int binarySearch(int arr[], int size, int key) {
    int low = 0, high = size - 1;
    while (low <= high) {
        int mid = (low + high) / 2;
        if (arr[mid] == key) return mid;
        if (arr[mid] < key) low = mid + 1;
        else high = mid - 1;
    }
    return -1;
}

int main() {
    int arr[] = {2, 3, 4, 10, 40};
    int size = sizeof(arr) / sizeof(arr[0]);
    int key = 10;
    int result = binarySearch(arr, size, key);
    if (result != -1) {
        printf("Element found at index %d\n", result);
    } else {
        printf("Element not found\n");
    }
    return 0;
}
```

OUTPUT
Element found at index 3

This program implements the **binary search algorithm** to find the position of a specified element (key) in a sorted array. Here's a step-by-step explanation of how it works:

Code Explanation
Step 1: Function Declaration

```
int binarySearch(int arr[], int size, int key)
```

- **arr[]**: The sorted array in which we are searching for the key.
- **size**: The number of elements in the array.
- **key**: The element we are trying to find.
- The function returns the index of key if found, otherwise returns -1.

Step 2: Initialize Variables

```
int low = 0, high = size - 1;
```

- **low**: The starting index of the array (initially 0).
- **high**: The ending index of the array (initially size - 1).

Step 3: Start Searching

The search is performed inside a while loop:

```
while (low <= high) {
```

The loop continues as long as there is a valid range to search (low <= high).

Step 4: Calculate the Middle Index

```
int mid = (low + high) / 2;
```

- The middle index is calculated as the average of low and high.
- For example:
  - If low = 0 and high = 4, then mid = (0 + 4) / 2 = 2.

Step 5: Compare the Middle Element

```
if (arr[mid] == key) return mid;
```

- If the element at the mid index matches the key, the search is successful, and the function returns mid (the index of the element).

Step 6: Narrow the Search Range

If the middle element is not the key:

1. **If the middle element is smaller than the key:**

```
if (arr[mid] < key) low = mid + 1;
```

- Discard the left half of the array (low becomes mid + 1).

2. **If the middle element is larger than the key:**

```
else high = mid - 1;
```

- Discard the right half of the array (high becomes mid - 1).

Step 7: Element Not Found

If the loop ends without finding the key, it means the element is not in the array:

```
return -1;
```

Step 8: Main Function

```
int arr[] = {2, 3, 4, 10, 40};
int size = sizeof(arr) / sizeof(arr[0]);
int key = 10;
```

- arr[]: The sorted array to search in.

- size: The size of the array (sizeof(arr) / sizeof(arr[0]) = 5).
- key: The element we are looking for (10 in this case).

Step 9: Call the Function

```
int result = binarySearch(arr, size, key);
```

- Calls the binarySearch function and stores the returned value (result).

Step 10: Check the Result

```
if (result != -1) {
    printf("Element found at index %d\n", result);
} else {
    printf("Element not found\n");
}
```

- If result != -1, print the index of the element.
- If result == -1, print "Element not found".

Execution Flow for key = 10

1. **Initialization**:
   - low = 0, high = 4 (indices of the array).
2. **1st Iteration**:
   - mid = (0 + 4) / 2 = 2.
   - arr[2] = 4 (less than 10).
   - Update: low = mid + 1 = 3.
3. **2nd Iteration**:
   - mid = (3 + 4) / 2 = 3.
   - arr[3] = 10 (equal to key).
   - Element found, return mid = 3.
4. **Output**:
   - "Element found at index 3".

6. Palindrome Check

Question: Write a C program to check if a string is a palindrome.

Answer:

```c
#include <stdio.h>
#include <string.h>
#include <ctype.h>

// Function to check if a string is a palindrome
int isPalindrome(char *str) {
    int n = strlen(str);
    for (int i = 0; i < n / 2; i++) {
        if (str[i] != str[n - i - 1]) return 0;
    }
    return 1;
}

// Function to remove newline and extra spaces
void preprocessString(char *str) {
    // Remove trailing newline character
    size_t len = strlen(str);
    if (len > 0 && str[len - 1] == '\n') {
        str[len - 1] = '\0';
    }

    // Optional: Convert to lowercase for case-insensitive check
    for (int i = 0; str[i]; i++) {
        str[i] = tolower(str[i]);
    }
}

int main() {
    char str[100];
    printf("Enter a string: ");
    if (fgets(str, sizeof(str), stdin)) {
```

```c
        preprocessString(str); // Clean the input
        if (isPalindrome(str)) {
            printf("\"%s\" is a palindrome\n", str);
        } else {
            printf("\"%s\" is not a palindrome\n", str);
        }
    } else {
        printf("Error reading input\n");
    }
    return 0;
}
```

OUTPUT
Enter a string: wow
"wow" is a palindrome

Let's break down your C code step by step:

1. #include Statements

These are preprocessor directives that include necessary header files:

- #include <stdio.h>: Includes standard input/output functions like printf() and fgets().
- #include <string.h>: Includes functions for string handling, like strlen().
- #include <ctype.h>: Includes functions for character handling, like tolower().

2. isPalindrome Function

This function checks if a string is a palindrome.

```c
int isPalindrome(char *str) {
    int n = strlen(str); // Get the length of the string
    for (int i = 0; i < n / 2; i++) { // Loop through the first half of the string
        if (str[i] != str[n - i - 1]) return 0; // If characters don't match, return 0 (false)
    }
```

```
    return 1; // Return 1 (true) if the string is a palindrome
}
```

- strlen(str) computes the length of the string str.
- A loop runs from the first character to the middle of the string (n / 2), comparing characters at opposite ends: str[i] and str[n - i - 1].
    - If any pair doesn't match, the function returns 0, indicating the string is **not** a palindrome.
    - If all pairs match, the function returns 1, meaning the string **is** a palindrome.

3. preprocessString Function

This function prepares the string for palindrome checking by removing trailing newlines and converting characters to lowercase (for case-insensitive comparison).

```
void preprocessString(char *str) {
    size_t len = strlen(str); // Get the length of the string
    if (len > 0 && str[len - 1] == '\n') { // Check if the string ends with a newline
        str[len - 1] = '\0'; // Replace newline with null terminator
    }

    // Convert all characters to lowercase
    for (int i = 0; str[i]; i++) {
        str[i] = tolower(str[i]); // Convert each character to lowercase
    }
}
```

- First, it checks if the string has a newline character (which is added by fgets() when reading input) at the end and removes it by replacing it with the null character ('\0').

- Then, the tolower() function is used to convert each character to lowercase. This ensures that the comparison for palindrome checking is **case-insensitive**.

4. main Function

This is where the program starts executing.

```c
int main() {
    char str[100]; // Declare a character array to store the input string
    printf("Enter a string: ");
    if (fgets(str, sizeof(str), stdin)) { // Read a line of input from the user
        preprocessString(str); // Clean the input by removing newline and converting to lowercase
        if (isPalindrome(str)) { // Check if the string is a palindrome
            printf("\"%s\" is a palindrome\n", str); // If yes, print that it's a palindrome
        } else {
            printf("\"%s\" is not a palindrome\n", str); // If no, print that it's not a palindrome
        }
    } else {
        printf("Error reading input\n"); // In case of an input error
    }
    return 0; // End of the program
}
```

- char str[100]: Declares a character array of size 100 to hold the user input.

- printf("Enter a string: ");: Prompts the user to enter a string.
- fgets(str, sizeof(str), stdin): Reads a line of text from standard input (up to 99 characters, leaving space for the null terminator). This is safer than scanf because it prevents buffer overflow.
    - If successful, the program proceeds to clean and check the input.
- preprocessString(str): Calls the preprocessing function to clean the string (remove the newline and convert to lowercase).
- isPalindrome(str): Calls the function to check if the string is a palindrome.
    - If the result is 1, the program prints that the string is a palindrome.
    - If the result is 0, the program prints that the string is not a palindrome.
- If fgets fails to read input (e.g., due to an error), the program prints an error message.

Key Concepts

- **Palindrome**: A string that reads the same forward and backward (e.g., "madam").
- **Case-insensitivity**: Ensuring the comparison of letters like 'a' and 'A' is treated the same.
- **String manipulation**: Using strlen() to find the string's length, tolower() to convert characters, and manipulating the string with basic array indexing.

7. Matrix Multiplication

Question: Write a C program to perform matrix multiplication.
Answer:

```
#include<stdio.h>
```

```c
int main() {
    int a[3][3], b[3][3], c[3][3] = {0};
    int i, j, k;

    printf("Enter elements of matrix A (3x3): ");
    for (i = 0; i < 3; i++) {
        for (j = 0; j < 3; j++) {
            scanf("%d", &a[i][j]);
        }
    }

    printf("Enter elements of matrix B (3x3): ");
    for (i = 0; i < 3; i++) {
        for (j = 0; j < 3; j++) {
            scanf("%d", &b[i][j]);
        }
    }

    // Matrix multiplication
    for (i = 0; i < 3; i++) {
        for (j = 0; j < 3; j++) {
            for (k = 0; k < 3; k++) {
                c[i][j] += a[i][k] * b[k][j];
            }
        }
    }

    printf("Resultant matrix C:\n");
    for (i = 0; i < 3; i++) {
        for (j = 0; j < 3; j++) {
            printf("%d ", c[i][j]);
        }
        printf("\n");
    }

    return 0;
```

```
}
```

OUTPUT
Enter elements of matrix A (3x3):
1 2 3
4 5 6
7 8 9

Enter elements of matrix B (3x3):
9 8 7
6 5 4
3 2 1

Resultant matrix C:
30   24 18
84   69 54
138 114 90

The C program you've provided multiplies two 3x3 matrices, A and B, and stores the result in matrix C. Let's go through it step by step:

1. Variable Declaration

```
int a[3][3], b[3][3], c[3][3] = {0};
int i, j, k;
```

- **a[3][3]**: This is a 3x3 matrix to store the elements of matrix A.
- **b[3][3]**: This is a 3x3 matrix to store the elements of matrix B.
- **c[3][3] = {0}**: This is a 3x3 matrix to store the result of matrix multiplication. It's initialized to all zeroes.
- **i, j, k**: These are integer variables used for iteration in the loops.

2. Input for Matrix A

```
printf("Enter elements of matrix A (3x3): ");
for (i = 0; i < 3; i++) {
```

```c
    for (j = 0; j < 3; j++) {
        scanf("%d", &a[i][j]);
    }
}
```

- The program prompts the user to enter the elements of matrix A.
- **scanf("%d", &a[i][j])** is used inside nested loops to fill the 3x3 matrix A with integers.

3. Input for Matrix B

```c
printf("Enter elements of matrix B (3x3): ");
for (i = 0; i < 3; i++) {
    for (j = 0; j < 3; j++) {
        scanf("%d", &b[i][j]);
    }
}
```

- Similar to matrix A, the program prompts the user to enter the elements for matrix B and stores them in matrix B using nested loops.

4. Matrix Multiplication

```c
for (i = 0; i < 3; i++) {
    for (j = 0; j < 3; j++) {
        for (k = 0; k < 3; k++) {
            c[i][j] += a[i][k] * b[k][j];
        }
    }
}
```

- The matrix multiplication process begins here.
- The outer two loops iterate over the rows of matrix A (denoted by i) and the columns of matrix B (denoted by j).

- The innermost loop iterates over the elements in the rows of A and columns of B (denoted by k), performing the necessary multiplication and addition.
    - **c[i][j] += a[i][k] * b[k][j];**: This calculates the element in the result matrix C by multiplying corresponding elements from matrix A and matrix B and adding them together.

5. Printing the Resultant Matrix

```
printf("Resultant matrix C:\n");
for (i = 0; i < 3; i++) {
   for (j = 0; j < 3; j++) {
      printf("%d ", c[i][j]);
   }
   printf("\n");
}
```

- This loop prints the resultant matrix C.
- The outer loop iterates over the rows of matrix C, and the inner loop iterates over the columns of matrix C, printing each element.

6. Return Statement

```
return 0;
```

- This line indicates the successful termination of the program and returns 0.

Summary of Matrix Multiplication:

Matrix multiplication follows the rule:

- If A is of size m×n and B is of size n×p, the resulting matrix C will have the dimensions m×p.
- For each element C[i][j], it is calculated as the sum of products:
C[i][j] = A[i][0] * B[0][j] + A[i][1] * B[1][j] + ... + A[i][n-1] * B[n-1][j].

Since you're multiplying two 3x3 matrices, the multiplication will compute the sum of products for each element in the result matrix.

Let's walk through an example input and output for your matrix multiplication program.

Example Input:

Matrix A:

```
1 2 3
4 5 6
7 8 9
```

Matrix B:

```
9 8 7
6 5 4
3 2 1
```

Matrix Multiplication Process:

The resultant matrix C is calculated as follows:

10. For C[0][0]: C[0][0]=(1*9)+(2*6)+(3*3)=9+12+9=30
11. For C[0][1]: C[0][1]=(1*8)+(2*5)+(3*2)=8+10+6=24
12. For C[0][2]: C[0][2]=(1*7)+(2*4)+(3*1)=7+8+3=18
13. For C[1][0]: C[1][0]=(4*9)+(5*6)+(6*3)=36+30+18=84
14. For C[1][1]: C[1][1]=(4*8)+(5*5)+(6*2)=32+25+12=69
15. For C[1][2]: C[1][2]=(4*7)+(5*4)+(6*1)=28+20+6=54
16. For C[2][0]: C[2][0]=(7*9)+(8*6)+(9*3)=63+48+27=138
17. For C[2][1]: C[2][1]=(7*8)+(8*5)+(9*2)=56+40+18=114
18. For C[2][2]: C[2][2] =(7*7)+(8*4)+(9*1)=49+32+9=90

Resultant Matrix C:

```
30  24  18
84  69  54
138 114 90
```

8. Find the Largest Element in an Array

Question: Write a C program to find the largest element in an array.

Answer:

```
#include <stdio.h>

int findLargest(int arr[], int n) {
    int max = arr[0];
    for (int i = 1; i < n; i++) {
        if (arr[i] > max) {
            max = arr[i];
        }
    }
    return max;
}

int main() {
    int arr[] = {1, 2, 3, 4, 5, 6, 7, 8, 9, 10};
    int n = sizeof(arr) / sizeof(arr[0]);
    int max = findLargest(arr, n);
    printf("The largest element is %d\n", max);
    return 0;
}
```

OUTPUT
The largest element is 10

Here's a step-by-step explanation of the provided C program:

Code Breakdown:

```
#include <stdio.h> // 1
```

- This includes the header file stdio.h which allows the program to use standard input and output functions, such as printf().

```
int findLargest(int arr[], int n) { // 2
    int max = arr[0]; // 3
    for (int i = 1; i < n; i++) { // 4
```

```
        if (arr[i] > max) {  // 5
            max = arr[i];  // 6
        }
    }
    return max;  // 7
}  // 8
```

- **Function Declaration (Line 2)**:
    - This defines a function findLargest that takes two arguments:
        - arr[]: an array of integers.
        - n: the number of elements in the array.
- **Initialization (Line 3)**:
    - A variable max is initialized to the first element of the array (arr[0]), assuming it is the largest value initially.
- **For Loop (Line 4)**:
    - The loop starts from the second element (i = 1) and iterates through the entire array. The loop will run n-1 times, where n is the size of the array.
- **Comparison (Line 5)**:
    - In each iteration, the element arr[i] is compared to the current max.
- **Updating max (Line 6)**:
    - If arr[i] is greater than the current value of max, the value of max is updated to arr[i].
- **Return Statement (Line 7)**:
    - After the loop completes, the function returns the largest element, stored in max.

```
int main() {  // 9
    int arr[] = {1, 2, 3, 4, 5, 6, 7, 8, 9, 10};  // 10
    int n = sizeof(arr) / sizeof(arr[0]);  // 11
    int max = findLargest(arr, n);  // 12
    printf("The largest element is %d\n", max);  // 13
```

```c
    return 0; // 14
}
```

- **main Function (Line 9):**
  - The main function serves as the entry point of the program.
- **Array Initialization (Line 10):**
  - An integer array arr[] is initialized with 10 elements: {1, 2, 3, 4, 5, 6, 7, 8, 9, 10}.
- **Array Size Calculation (Line 11):**
  - n is calculated by dividing the total size of the array arr (sizeof(arr)) by the size of a single element (sizeof(arr[0])). This gives the number of elements in the array.
- **Function Call (Line 12):**
  - The findLargest function is called with the array arr and its size n. The returned value (largest element) is stored in the variable max.
- **Printing the Result (Line 13):**
  - The largest element max is printed to the console using printf(). The output format is: The largest element is <max>, where <max> is the value returned by the findLargest function.
- **Program End (Line 14):**
  - The main function returns 0, indicating successful execution of the program.

Execution Flow:

1. The program starts execution from main().
2. The array arr[] is created and filled with values from 1 to 10.
3. The findLargest() function is called with arr[] and its size n (10).
4. Inside findLargest(), the largest element is found by iterating over the array and comparing each element

with the current maximum value (max).
5. The largest element is returned from findLargest().
6. The largest element is printed in main().
7. The program ends, and the output is displayed on the screen.

9. Check for Armstrong Number

Question: Write a C program to check if a given number is an Armstrong number.

Answer:

```c
#include <stdio.h>
#include <math.h>

int isArmstrong(int num) {
    int originalNum, remainder, result = 0, n = 0;
    originalNum = num;
    while (originalNum != 0) {
        originalNum /= 10;
        ++n;
    }
    originalNum = num;
    while (originalNum != 0) {
        remainder = originalNum % 10;
        result += pow(remainder, n);
        originalNum /= 10;
    }
    return result == num;
}
int main() {
    int num;
    printf("Enter a number: ");
    scanf("%d", &num);
    if (isArmstrong(num)) {
        printf("%d is an Armstrong number\n", num);
```

```
    } else {
        printf("%d is not an Armstrong number\n", num);
    }
    return 0;
}
```

OUTPUT
Enter a number: 153
153 is an Armstrong number

Enter a number: 123
123 is not an Armstrong number

This C program checks if a given number is an Armstrong number. An Armstrong number (also called a narcissistic number) is a number that is equal to the sum of its own digits each raised to the power of the number of digits.

Here's a detailed breakdown of the program:

1. isArmstrong Function:

This function determines whether the number passed to it (num) is an Armstrong number.

```
int isArmstrong(int num) {
    int originalNum, remainder, result = 0, n = 0;
    originalNum = num;
```

- originalNum: A variable that holds the original number for manipulation.
- remainder: A variable used to store the last digit of originalNum when extracted.
- result: The variable to store the sum of the digits raised to the power of n.
- n: The number of digits in the original number.

```
while (originalNum != 0) {
    originalNum /= 10;
    ++n;
```

```
    }
```

- This loop calculates the number of digits (n) in the input number (num) by repeatedly dividing the number by 10. The number of iterations gives the number of digits.

```
    originalNum = num;
    while (originalNum != 0) {
        remainder = originalNum % 10;
        result += pow(remainder, n);
        originalNum /= 10;
    }
```

This loop extracts each digit of num starting from the last digit (remainder = originalNum % 10) and adds the digit raised to the power of n to the result variable.

- pow(remainder, n) computes the digit raised to the power of n (the number of digits).
- The number is then reduced by removing the last digit using originalNum /= 10.

```
    return result == num;
}
```

- Finally, the function checks if the result (sum of digits raised to the power of n) is equal to the original number. If they are equal, the number is an Armstrong number, so the function returns 1 (true); otherwise, it returns 0 (false).

2. main Function:

```
int main() {
    int num;
    printf("Enter a number: ");
    scanf("%d", &num);
```

- The program asks the user to enter a number (num) using printf and scanf.

```
if (isArmstrong(num)) {
    printf("%d is an Armstrong number\n", num);
} else {
    printf("%d is not an Armstrong number\n", num);
}
```

- The program calls the isArmstrong function with the entered number. If it returns 1 (true), the program prints that the number is an Armstrong number; otherwise, it prints that it is not.

Example:

For example, if you enter 153:
- It has 3 digits (so n = 3).
- The Armstrong check is: $1^3 + 5^3 + 3^3 = 1 + 125 + 27 = 153$
- Since the sum equals the original number, it will print "153 is an Armstrong number."

If you enter 123:
- It has 3 digits (so n = 3).
- The Armstrong check is: $1^3 + 2^3 + 3^3 = 1 + 8 + 27 = 36$
- Since the sum does not equal the original number, it will print "123 is not an Armstrong number."

10. Count the Number of Vowels in a String

Question: Write a C program to count the number of vowels in a given string.

Answer:

```c
#include <stdio.h>
```

```c
#include <string.h>

int countVowels(char *str) {
    int count = 0;
    for (int i = 0; str[i] != '\0'; i++) {
        if (str[i] == 'a' || str[i] == 'e' || str[i] == 'i' || str[i] == 'o' || str[i] == 'u' ||
            str[i] == 'A' || str[i] == 'E' || str[i] == 'I' || str[i] == 'O' || str[i] == 'U') {
            count++;
        }
    }
    return count;
}

int main() {
    char str[100];
    printf("Enter a string: ");

    // Use fgets to safely read input
    fgets(str, sizeof(str), stdin);

    // Remove newline character if it exists at the end of the string
    str[strcspn(str, "\n")] = '\0';

    printf("Number of vowels: %d\n", countVowels(str));
    return 0;
}
```

OUTPUT
Enter a string: hello world
Number of vowels: 3

This C program counts the number of vowels (both lowercase and uppercase) in a user-provided string. Here's a step-by-step breakdown:

1. Function Definition: countVowels

```c
int countVowels(char *str) {
    int count = 0;
    for (int i = 0; str[i] != '\0'; i++) {
        if (str[i] == 'a' || str[i] == 'e' || str[i] == 'i' || str[i] == 'o' || str[i] == 'u' ||
            str[i] == 'A' || str[i] == 'E' || str[i] == 'I' || str[i] == 'O' || str[i] == 'U') {
            count++;
        }
    }
    return count;
}
```

- **Input:** A string str (character array).
- **Logic:**
  - count: A variable initialized to 0 that will keep track of the number of vowels.
  - The program loops through each character of the string until it encounters the null terminator \0, which marks the end of the string.
  - Inside the loop, it checks if the current character is a vowel (either uppercase or lowercase) using the if statement.
  - If it is a vowel, count is incremented by 1.
- **Output:** The function returns the total number of vowels found in the string.

2. Main Function:

```c
int main() {
    char str[100];
    printf("Enter a string: ");

    // Use fgets to safely read input
    fgets(str, sizeof(str), stdin);
```

```
    // Remove newline character if it exists at the end of the
string
    str[strcspn(str, "\n")] = '\0';

    printf("Number of vowels: %d\n", countVowels(str));
    return 0;
}
```

- **Input:**
    - A string entered by the user.
- **Logic:**
    - A character array str[100] is declared to store the input string. The size of 100 is enough to store typical user input.
    - fgets is used to safely read the input string, allowing for spaces and ensuring the input does not exceed 99 characters (the extra 1 is for the null terminator).
    - strcspn(str, "\n") is used to find the index of the newline character \n that fgets adds at the end of the string when the user presses Enter. If a newline exists, it is replaced by a null terminator \0 to clean up the string.
- **Output:**
    - The countVowels function is called to count the number of vowels in the string, and the result is printed.

Example Walkthrough:

If the user inputs the string Hello World, the program:

1. Reads the input Hello World.
2. Counts the vowels:
    - 'e' (vowel)
    - 'o' (vowel)
    - 'o' (vowel)
    - Total vowels = 3.

3. Outputs: Number of vowels: 3.

11. Merge Two Sorted Arrays

Question: Write a C program to merge two sorted arrays into a single sorted array.

Answer:

```
#include <stdio.h>

void mergeArrays(int arr1[], int arr2[], int n1, int n2, int arr3[]) {
    int i = 0, j = 0, k = 0;
    while (i < n1 && j < n2) {
        if (arr1[i] < arr2[j]) {
            arr3[k++] = arr1[i++];
        } else {
            arr3[k++] = arr2[j++];
        }
    }
    while (i < n1) {
        arr3[k++] = arr1[i++];
    }
    while (j < n2) {
        arr3[k++] = arr2[j++];
    }
}

int main() {
    int arr1[] = {1, 3, 5, 7};
    int arr2[] = {2, 4, 6, 8};
    int n1 = sizeof(arr1) / sizeof(arr1[0]);
    int n2 = sizeof(arr2) / sizeof(arr2[0]);
    int arr3[n1 + n2];

    mergeArrays(arr1, arr2, n1, n2, arr3);

    printf("Merged array: ");
```

```c
    for (int i = 0; i < n1 + n2; i++) {
        printf("%d ", arr3[i]);
    }
    printf("\n");
    return 0;
}
```

OUTPUT
Merged array: 1 2 3 4 5 6 7 8

This C code merges two sorted arrays into a third array while maintaining the order. Let's break it down step by step:

1. Function Definition: mergeArrays

```c
void mergeArrays(int arr1[], int arr2[], int n1, int n2, int arr3[]) {
```

- This function takes five parameters:
    - arr1[]: The first input array.
    - arr2[]: The second input array.
    - n1: The size of arr1.
    - n2: The size of arr2.
    - arr3[]: The resulting array where the merged elements will be stored.

2. Initial Variable Setup

```c
int i = 0, j = 0, k = 0;
```

- i, j, and k are index variables:
    - i tracks the current position in arr1.
    - j tracks the current position in arr2.
    - k tracks the current position in arr3 where the next smallest element will be placed.

3. Merging Arrays

```c
while (i < n1 && j < n2) {
    if (arr1[i] < arr2[j]) {
        arr3[k++] = arr1[i++];
```

```
    } else {
        arr3[k++] = arr2[j++];
    }
}
```

- The while loop runs as long as there are still elements in both arr1 and arr2 to compare.
- Inside the loop, the smaller of the two elements arr1[i] or arr2[j] is placed in arr3[k]. Then, the respective index (i or j) and the index k are incremented.
    - If arr1[i] is smaller than arr2[j], arr1[i] is added to arr3[k], and i and k are incremented.
    - Otherwise, arr2[j] is added to arr3[k], and j and k are incremented.

4. Handling Remaining Elements

After the first loop, one of the arrays may still have elements left. To handle this:

- **Copy remaining elements from arr1:**

```
while (i < n1) {
    arr3[k++] = arr1[i++];
}
```

- If there are elements left in arr1 (i.e., i < n1), they are copied to arr3 in order.
- **Copy remaining elements from arr2:**

```
while (j < n2) {
    arr3[k++] = arr2[j++];
}
```

- If there are elements left in arr2 (i.e., j < n2), they are copied to arr3 in order.

5. Main Function: Merging and Printing

```
int main() {
    int arr1[] = {1, 3, 5, 7};
    int arr2[] = {2, 4, 6, 8};
    int n1 = sizeof(arr1) / sizeof(arr1[0]);
    int n2 = sizeof(arr2) / sizeof(arr2[0]);
    int arr3[n1 + n2];
```

- arr1[] and arr2[] are the two sorted input arrays.
- n1 and n2 are computed as the number of elements in arr1 and arr2 by dividing the total size of the array by the size of a single element (sizeof(arr1[0])).
- arr3[] is declared to hold the merged result. Its size is the sum of the sizes of arr1 and arr2.

```
mergeArrays(arr1, arr2, n1, n2, arr3);
```

- The mergeArrays function is called to merge arr1[] and arr2[] into arr3[].

```
printf("Merged array: ");
for (int i = 0; i < n1 + n2; i++) {
    printf("%d ", arr3[i]);
}
printf("\n");
```

- A loop prints the elements of arr3[], which now contains the merged and sorted elements from both arr1[] and arr2[].

12. Sum of Digits of a Number

Question: Write a C program to find the sum of digits of a given number.

Answer:

```
#include <stdio.h>
```

```
int sumOfDigits(int num) {
    int sum = 0;
    while (num != 0) {
        sum += num % 10;
        num /= 10;
    }
    return sum;
}

int main() {
    int num;
    printf("Enter a number: ");
    scanf("%d", &num);
    printf("Sum of digits: %d\n", sumOfDigits(num));
    return 0;
}
```

OUTPUT
Enter a number: 1234
Sum of digits: 10

The given C program calculates the sum of the digits of a number. Let's go through the code step by step:

1. Include Header File

```
#include <stdio.h>
```

- This line includes the standard input-output header file (stdio.h) to enable the program to use functions like printf and scanf for printing to the console and reading input from the user.

2. Function Definition - sumOfDigits

```
int sumOfDigits(int num) {
    int sum = 0;
    while (num != 0) {
        sum += num % 10;
```

```
        num /= 10;
    }
    return sum;
}
```

- **int sumOfDigits(int num)**: This is a function that takes an integer num as input and returns the sum of its digits.

Inside the function:

- **int sum = 0;**: A variable sum is declared and initialized to 0. This variable will hold the sum of the digits.
- **while (num != 0)**: The while loop continues until num becomes 0. In each iteration, it processes one digit of the number.
  - **num % 10**: This operation extracts the last digit of num. For example, if num is 1234, 1234 % 10 will give 4.
  - **sum += num % 10;**: The extracted digit is added to the sum. So, in the first iteration, if num = 1234, sum will be 4 after this operation.
  - **num /= 10;**: This operation removes the last digit from num. For example, 1234 / 10 will result in 123. This process continues in each iteration, reducing the number by one digit at a time.
- **return sum;**: After the loop finishes (when num becomes 0), the function returns the final value of sum, which is the sum of the digits of the original number.

3. Main Function

```
int main() {
    int num;
    printf("Enter a number: ");
    scanf("%d", &num);
```

```
printf("Sum of digits: %d\n", sumOfDigits(num));
return 0;
}
```

- **int num;:** A variable num is declared to store the number entered by the user.
- **printf("Enter a number: ");:** This prints a message to the console asking the user to enter a number.
- **scanf("%d", &num);:** This reads the integer input from the user and stores it in the variable num.
- **printf("Sum of digits: %d\n", sumOfDigits(num));:** This calls the function sumOfDigits(num) to calculate the sum of the digits of num, and then prints the result to the console.
- **return 0;:** This statement indicates that the program executed successfully and ends the main function.

Example Walkthrough

Suppose the user enters the number 1234.

- **First iteration:**
    - num = 1234
    - num % 10 = 4 (last digit)
    - sum += 4 → sum = 4
    - num /= 10 → num = 123
- **Second iteration:**
    - num = 123
    - num % 10 = 3 (last digit)
    - sum += 3 → sum = 7
    - num /= 10 → num = 12
- **Third iteration:**
    - num = 12
    - num % 10 = 2 (last digit)
    - sum += 2 → sum = 9

- num /= 10 → num = 1
- **Fourth iteration:**
  - num = 1
  - num % 10 = 1 (last digit)
  - sum += 1 → sum = 10
  - num /= 10 → num = 0 (loop ends)

The function returns 10, which is the sum of the digits of 1234.

13. Find GCD of Two Numbers

Question: Write a C program to find the greatest common divisor (GCD) of two numbers.

Answer:

```c
#include <stdio.h>

int gcd(int a, int b) {
    if (b == 0)
        return a;
    return gcd(b, a % b);
}

int main() {
    int a, b;
    printf("Enter two numbers: ");
    scanf("%d %d", &a, &b);
    printf("GCD of %d and %d is %d\n", a, b, gcd(a, b));
    return 0;
}
```

OUTPUT
Enter two numbers: 56 98
GCD of 56 and 98 is 14

This program calculates the **Greatest Common Divisor (GCD)** of two numbers using the **Euclidean algorithm**. Let's go step by step through the code:

1. Header file inclusion:

```c
#include <stdio.h>
```

- **#include <stdio.h>**: This line includes the standard input/output library. It allows the program to use functions like printf (for printing output) and scanf (for reading input).

2. Function to calculate GCD:

```c
int gcd(int a, int b) {
    if (b == 0)
        return a;
    return gcd(b, a % b);
}
```

- **gcd(int a, int b)**: This is a recursive function that calculates the GCD of two integers a and b.
  - **Base Case:**

```c
if (b == 0)
    return a;
```

  - The Euclidean algorithm for GCD states that if one of the numbers becomes 0, the other number is the GCD. If b == 0, the function returns a as the result.
  - **Recursive Case:**

```c
return gcd(b, a % b);
```

  - If b != 0, the function recursively calls itself with b and a % b (the remainder when a is divided by b). This process repeats until b becomes 0, at which point the base case is triggered.

3. Main Function:

```c
int main() {
```

```
    int a, b;
    printf("Enter two numbers: ");
    scanf("%d %d", &a, &b);
    printf("GCD of %d and %d is %d\n", a, b, gcd(a, b));
    return 0;
}
```

- **Variable Declaration:**

```
int a, b;
```

  - This declares two integer variables a and b to store the two numbers whose GCD will be calculated.

- **Input Prompt:**

```
printf("Enter two numbers: ");
```

  - This prints a prompt asking the user to enter two numbers.

- **Reading Input:**

```
scanf("%d %d", &a, &b);
```

  - This reads two integers entered by the user and stores them in variables a and b.

- **Calling gcd Function:**

```
printf("GCD of %d and %d is %d\n", a, b, gcd(a, b));
```

  - The gcd(a, b) function is called with the user-entered values of a and b. The result is printed in the format "GCD of a and b is result".

How the Euclidean Algorithm Works (Example):

Suppose the user enters a = 56 and b = 98:

- First, the function is called with gcd(56, 98).

- Since 98 != 0, the function calls gcd(98, 56 % 98) → gcd(98, 56).
- Now gcd(98, 56) calls gcd(56, 98 % 56) → gcd(56, 42).
- Now gcd(56, 42) calls gcd(42, 56 % 42) → gcd(42, 14).
- Now gcd(42, 14) calls gcd(14, 42 % 14) → gcd(14, 0).
- Since b == 0, the base case returns 14, which is the GCD.

14. Sort an Array

Question: Write a C program to sort an array using bubble sort.

Answer:

```
#include <stdio.h>
void bubbleSort(int arr[], int n) {
    for (int i = 0; i < n - 1; i++) {
        for (int j = 0; j < n - i - 1; j++) {
            if (arr[j] > arr[j + 1]) {
                int temp = arr[j];
                arr[j] = arr[j + 1];
                arr[j + 1] = temp;
            }
        }
    }
}
int main() {
    int arr[] = {64, 34, 25, 12, 22, 11, 90};
    int n = sizeof(arr) / sizeof(arr[0]);
    bubbleSort(arr, n);
    printf("Sorted array: ");
    for (int i = 0; i < n; i++) {
        printf("%d ", arr[i]);
    }
    printf("\n");
    return 0;
```

```
}
```

OUTPUT
Sorted array: 11 12 22 25 34 64 90

This C program implements the **Bubble Sort** algorithm to sort an array of integers. Let's go through it step by step.

1. Header Files and Function Declaration

```
#include <stdio.h>
```

- This line includes the standard input-output library (stdio.h), which allows the program to use functions like printf to display output.

2. Bubble Sort Function

```
void bubbleSort(int arr[], int n) {
    for (int i = 0; i < n - 1; i++) {
        for (int j = 0; j < n - i - 1; j++) {
            if (arr[j] > arr[j + 1]) {
                int temp = arr[j];
                arr[j] = arr[j + 1];
                arr[j + 1] = temp;
            }
        }
    }
}
```

- This function sorts the array using the **Bubble Sort** algorithm.
- **Arguments**:
    - arr[]: The array to be sorted.
    - n: The size of the array.

Explanation of the Loop:

- **Outer Loop (for (int i = 0; i < n - 1; i++))**: This loop runs n - 1 times. Each pass of the outer loop ensures that the largest element of the unsorted part of the array

"bubbles" up to its correct position.
- **Inner Loop (for (int j = 0; j < n - i - 1; j++))**:
    - This loop compares adjacent elements in the array. The number of comparisons decreases with each iteration of the outer loop because the largest elements have already been placed at the end of the array.
    - **Swap Logic**: If arr[j] > arr[j + 1], it swaps the two elements. This swap is done using a temporary variable temp:
        - int temp = arr[j]; stores the value of arr[j] in temp.
        - arr[j] = arr[j + 1]; assigns the value of arr[j + 1] to arr[j].
        - arr[j + 1] = temp; assigns the value of temp (which was the original arr[j]) to arr[j + 1].
- As a result, after each pass of the outer loop, the largest element in the unsorted section of the array is placed in its correct position at the end.

3. Main Function

```
int main() {
    int arr[] = {64, 34, 25, 12, 22, 11, 90};
    int n = sizeof(arr) / sizeof(arr[0]);
    bubbleSort(arr, n);
    printf("Sorted array: ");
    for (int i = 0; i < n; i++) {
        printf("%d ", arr[i]);
    }
    printf("\n");
    return 0;
}
```

- **Array Initialization**: int arr[] = {64, 34, 25, 12, 22, 11, 90};

- An array arr is initialized with some unsorted integers.
- **Finding the Array Size**: int n = sizeof(arr) / sizeof(arr[0]);
  - The size of the array is calculated by dividing the total size of the array (sizeof(arr)) by the size of a single element (sizeof(arr[0])).
  - This gives the total number of elements in the array (n).
- **Calling the bubbleSort Function**: bubbleSort(arr, n);
  - The bubbleSort function is called to sort the array arr using the size n.
- **Printing the Sorted Array**:
  - The program prints the sorted array using a for loop:

```
for (int i = 0; i < n; i++) {
   printf("%d ", arr[i]);
}
```

- This loop prints each element of the array separated by a space.
- **Final Output**: After the loop, printf("\n"); adds a new line after printing the sorted array.
- **Return Statement**: return 0;
  - The main function returns 0, signaling successful execution of the program.

4. Bubble Sort Steps (Example)

Given the initial array:

Copy code

{64, 34, 25, 12, 22, 11, 90}

Pass 1 (i = 0):

- Compare 64 and 34, swap: {34, 64, 25, 12, 22, 11, 90}
- Compare 64 and 25, swap: {34, 25, 64, 12, 22, 11, 90}

- Compare 64 and 12, swap: {34, 25, 12, 64, 22, 11, 90}
- Compare 64 and 22, swap: {34, 25, 12, 22, 64, 11, 90}
- Compare 64 and 11, swap: {34, 25, 12, 22, 11, 64, 90}
- Compare 64 and 90, no swap: {34, 25, 12, 22, 11, 64, 90}

At the end of the first pass, 64 is at the correct position.

Pass 2 (i = 1):

- Compare 34 and 25, swap: {25, 34, 12, 22, 11, 64, 90}
- Compare 34 and 12, swap: {25, 12, 34, 22, 11, 64, 90}
- Compare 34 and 22, swap: {25, 12, 22, 34, 11, 64, 90}
- Compare 34 and 11, swap: {25, 12, 22, 11, 34, 64, 90}
- Compare 34 and 64, no swap: {25, 12, 22, 11, 34, 64, 90}

At the end of this pass, 34 is at the correct position.

This process continues until all elements are sorted. By the end of the final pass, the array will be completely sorted as {11, 12, 22, 25, 34, 64, 90}.

15. Check if a Number is a Power of Two

Question: Write a C program to check if a given number is a power of two.

Answer:

```
#include <stdio.h>

int isPowerOfTwo(int n) {
   if (n == 0)
      return 0;
   while (n != 1) {
      if (n % 2 != 0)
         return 0;
      n = n / 2;
   }
   return 1;
}
```

```c
int main() {
    int num;
    printf("Enter a number: ");
    scanf("%d", &num);
    if (isPowerOfTwo(num)) {
        printf("%d is a power of two\n", num);
    } else {
        printf("%d is not a power of two\n", num);
    }
    return 0;
}
```

OUTPUT
Enter a number: 16
16 is a power of two

The code determines whether a given number is a power of two. A number is a power of two if it can be expressed as 2^n, where n is a non-negative integer (e.g., 1, 2, 4, 8, 16, 32, etc.).

Detailed Breakdown:

1. Function Declaration:

```c
int isPowerOfTwo(int n) {
```

- A function isPowerOfTwo is declared, which takes an integer n and returns an integer (0 or 1), indicating whether the number is a power of two.

2. Handling Special Case:

```c
if (n == 0)
    return 0;
```

- The function checks if n is 0. Zero is not a power of two, so it immediately returns 0 (false).

3. While Loop:

```c
while (n != 1) {
```

- The loop will continue until n becomes 1, as any power of two can eventually be reduced to 1 by repeatedly dividing by 2.

4. Checking for Odd Numbers:

```
if (n % 2 != 0)
    return 0;
```

- The condition n % 2 != 0 checks if n is odd (not divisible by 2). If it is, the function returns 0 because an odd number cannot be a power of two (powers of two are always even except for 1).

5. Dividing by 2:

```
n = n / 2;
```

- If n is even, the program divides n by 2 and continues the loop. The process will eventually reduce powers of two to 1.

6. Returning True:

```
return 1;
```

- If the loop successfully reduces n to 1, it means that the number was a power of two, and the function returns 1 (true).

Main Function:
7. Reading Input:

```
int num;
printf("Enter a number: ");
scanf("%d", &num);
```

- The program declares an integer num and prompts the

user to input a number using scanf. The value entered is stored in num.

8. Checking for Power of Two:

```
if (isPowerOfTwo(num)) {
```

- The program calls the isPowerOfTwo function to check whether the input number is a power of two. If it returns 1, it means the number is a power of two.

9. Displaying Result:

```
printf("%d is a power of two\n", num);
```

- If the number is a power of two, it prints that the number is a power of two.

10. Else Case:

```
} else {
    printf("%d is not a power of two\n", num);
}
```

- If the number is not a power of two, it prints that the number is not a power of two.

11. Program Exit:

return 0;

- The program exits successfully, returning 0.

Example Execution:

Let's say the user inputs 16.

1. isPowerOfTwo(16) is called.
2. The function checks if n is 0 (it's not).
3. Then, it enters the while loop and repeatedly divides 16 by 2:
   - First, 16 % 2 == 0, so 16 / 2 = 8.
   - Then, 8 % 2 == 0, so 8 / 2 = 4.

- Then, 4 % 2 == 0, so 4 / 2 = 2.
- Then, 2 % 2 == 0, so 2 / 2 = 1.

4. Since n is now 1, the function returns 1, indicating that 16 is a power of two.
5. The main function prints 16 is a power of two.

16. Write a c program to demonstrate malloc() and free().

Answer:

```
#include <stdio.h>
#include <stdlib.h>

int main() {
   int n, *arr;
   printf("Enter number of elements: ");
   scanf("%d", &n);

   arr = (int *)malloc(n * sizeof(int)); // Memory allocation
   if (arr == NULL) {
      printf("Memory not allocated.\n");
      return 1;
   }

   printf("Enter %d elements: ", n);
   for (int i = 0; i < n; i++) {
      scanf("%d", &arr[i]);
   }

   printf("Elements are: ");
   for (int i = 0; i < n; i++) {
      printf("%d ", arr[i]);
   }

   free(arr); // Deallocate memory
   return 0;
}
```

OUTPUT

```
Enter number of elements: 5
Enter 5 elements: 1
2
3
4
5
Elements are: 1 2 3 4 5
```

The C program provided dynamically allocates memory for an array based on user input, stores elements in that array, and then deallocates the memory when done. Here's a step-by-step explanation of the program:

1. Include Libraries:

```
#include <stdio.h>
#include <stdlib.h>
```

- stdio.h is included to use input/output functions like printf() and scanf().
- stdlib.h is included for memory management functions like malloc() and free().

2. Define the main function:

```
int main() {
```

This is the entry point of the program.

3. Declare Variables:

```
int n, *arr;
```

- n: This variable will hold the number of elements the user wants to enter into the array.
- arr: This is a pointer to an integer, which will point to the dynamically allocated memory for the array.

4. Prompt User for Number of Elements:

```
printf("Enter number of elements: ");
```

```
scanf("%d", &n);
```

- The program asks the user to input the number of elements (n) they want to store in the array.
- The scanf function is used to read this input and store it in the variable n.

5. Dynamically Allocate Memory:

```
arr = (int *)malloc(n * sizeof(int)); // Memory allocation
```

- malloc() is used to allocate memory dynamically. It reserves space for n integers (because the size of an integer is platform-dependent, sizeof(int) is used to ensure the correct size).
- malloc returns a pointer to the allocated memory, which is cast to int* and assigned to arr.
- If the allocation fails (e.g., due to insufficient memory), malloc() returns NULL.

6. Check Memory Allocation:

```
if (arr == NULL) {
   printf("Memory not allocated.\n");
   return 1;
}
```

- This if statement checks if memory allocation was successful.
- If arr is NULL, it means memory allocation failed, and an error message is printed. The program then returns 1 to indicate an error and exits.

7. Prompt User to Enter Array Elements:

```
printf("Enter %d elements: ", n);
for (int i = 0; i < n; i++) {
   scanf("%d", &arr[i]);
```

```
}
```

- The program asks the user to input n elements for the array.
- The for loop runs from 0 to n-1, and inside the loop, each element of the array is entered using scanf().

8. Display the Elements of the Array:

```
printf("Elements are: ");
for (int i = 0; i < n; i++) {
   printf("%d ", arr[i]);
}
```

- After inputting the elements, the program prints the array elements using another for loop.
- Each element of the array is accessed using the pointer arr[i].

9. Deallocate Memory:

```
free(arr); // Deallocate memory
```

- free() is used to release the memory that was dynamically allocated for the array. It helps avoid memory leaks by freeing up resources that are no longer needed.

10. Return Statement:

```
return 0;
```

- This returns 0 to the operating system, signaling that the program executed successfully.

Summary of Program Execution:

1. The program first asks for the number of elements.
2. It dynamically allocates memory for the array based on the user's input.

3. The program prompts the user to input the array elements.
4. It displays the entered elements.
5. Finally, it deallocates the memory before terminating.

17. Star Pattern Program in C (Right-Angled Triangle)

```c
#include <stdio.h>

int main() {
    int i, j, n;

    // Input number of rows
    printf("Enter the number of rows: ");
    scanf("%d", &n);

    // Outer loop for rows
    for (i = 1; i <= n; i++) {
        // Inner loop for printing stars
        for (j = 1; j <= i; j++) {
            printf("* ");
        }
        printf("\n");
    }

    return 0;
}
```

OUTPUT
Enter the number of rows: 5
*
* *
* * *
* * * *
* * * * *

This C program prints a right-angled triangle pattern using stars (*). Let's go through the code step by step to understand how it works.

1. Include the necessary header file

```c
#include <stdio.h>
```

This line includes the Standard Input Output library (stdio.h), which allows the program to use functions like printf and scanf for input and output operations.

2. Define the main function

```
int main() {
```

The main() function is where the execution of the program begins.

3. Declare the variables

c
Copy code
```
int i, j, n;
```

- i: Used to control the outer loop (the rows).
- j: Used to control the inner loop (the stars printed in each row).
- n: Used to store the number of rows the user wants for the pattern.

4. Input the number of rows

```
printf("Enter the number of rows: ");
scanf("%d", &n);
```

- printf displays the message "Enter the number of rows: ".
- scanf reads the user's input and stores it in the variable n.

5. Outer loop for rows

```
for (i = 1; i <= n; i++) {
```

This outer loop runs n times. It controls the number of rows printed. The loop starts with i = 1 and continues until i equals n. Each iteration of this loop corresponds to printing a new row.

6. Inner loop for printing stars

```
for (j = 1; j <= i; j++) {
    printf("* ");
}
```

- The inner loop runs i times in each iteration of the outer loop. This is where the stars (*) are printed.
- On the first iteration (i = 1), the inner loop runs once and prints 1 star.
- On the second iteration (i = 2), the inner loop runs twice and prints 2 stars.
- On the third iteration (i = 3), the inner loop runs three times, and so on.

- printf("* ") prints a star followed by a space. This space is important to separate the stars visually.

7. Print a newline after each row

```
printf("\n");
```

After the inner loop finishes printing the stars for the current row, this line ensures that the program moves to the next line to print the stars for the next row.

8. End of loops and main function

c
Copy code
return 0;

- return 0 indicates that the program has finished successfully. It ends the main function and returns control to the operating system.

Star Pyramid Pattern Program in C

```c
#include <stdio.h>

int main() {
    int i, j, k, n;

    // Input number of rows for the pyramid
    printf("Enter the number of rows: ");
    scanf("%d", &n);

    // Outer loop for rows
    for (i = 1; i <= n; i++) {
        // Print spaces before stars for proper alignment
        for (j = 1; j <= n - i; j++) {
            printf(" ");
        }

        // Print stars
        for (k = 1; k <= (2 * i - 1); k++) {
            printf("*");
        }

        // Move to the next line after each row
```

```
        printf("\n");
    }
    return 0;
}
```

OUTPUT
Enter the number of rows: 5
```
    *
   ***
  *****
 *******
*********
```

Explanation:

1. The outer loop (i loop) controls the number of rows in the pyramid.
2. The first inner loop (j loop) prints spaces. The number of spaces decreases as the number of rows increases, ensuring the pyramid is centered.
3. The second inner loop (k loop) prints stars. The number of stars increases in each row, starting from 1 and increasing by 2 for each subsequent row.
4. After printing spaces and stars for each row, a new line is printed to move to the next row.

www.ingramcontent.com/pod-product-compliance
Lightning Source LLC
Chambersburg PA
CBHW071028240526
45469CB00006BD/2130